LOVE
FOR
ALL
YOUR
WORTH

LOVE FOR ALL YOUR WORTH

A Quest For Personal Value And Lovability

Joseph C. Aldrich

MULTNOMAH · PRESS
Portland, Oregon 97266

CONTENTS

INTRODUCTION 7

PART 1
TRANSFORMING YOURSELF:
THE INSIDE STORY

1   Discovering a Valuable Purpose 13
2   Discerning Your Ultimate Value 25
3   Developing Your Practical Value 41
4   Restoring Your Conscience 51
5   Responding to Your Conscience 63

PART 2
TRANSFORMING YOUR WORLD:
THE REST OF THE STORY

6   Love Encourages Growth 77
7   Love Fortifies Truth 89
8   Love Drives Out Fear 103
9   Love Builds Character 113
10 Love's Pilgrimage 125

INTRODUCTION

Somehow the term *lovable* doesn't mix well with grime, grease, dirt, blood, sweat, and tears. It doesn't come across as an idea . . . a reality . . . a victory forged out of the toughest challenge, the most difficult circumstances, the times of despair.

Has the quest to become lovable been evacuated of meaning? Have the word-snatchers struck again?

Looks to me like the teddy bears and velveteen bunnies waltzed off with *lovable*. Kidnaped it, to be exact. Housewives, truck drivers, lift operators, miners . . . folks of every flavor . . . have been robbed. I've filed a missing-term report. It's serious.

Exactly when the snatch took place is hard to determine. These losses don't always show up right away. The targeted terms are gradually taken out of context—until there's nothing left to take. They're gone. How long has it been since you used *lovable* . . . outside the toy store? I'd wager when you think of *lovable* you see dolls, stuffed animals, and chubby, jolly, rosy-cheeked folks sipping lemonade. I knew it.

The word-robbers have emasculated a strong, lean, muscular term. What they left in its place is hardly worth talking about: a spongy, pillowy, perfumey thing—a tablespoon of saccharin—twenty-four hours of elevator music. What a travesty!

Let me ask you a question. Are you consciously working at becoming more lovable? Cast ballet slippers, silk ribbons, and fuzzy, stuffed Garfield toys from your mind.

7

INTRODUCTION

You've been robbed. To become more lovable is the greatest challenge you will ever face. It is the greatest test of your courage and faith. The real measure of your success.

Let's back into this again. Deep down in your heart of hearts, don't you really long to be perceived by friends, associates, and family as someone who is lovable? This is something more than simply performing "actions of love." It's immeasurably beyond being a "good-deed doer." We're talking about an individual whom people love to love. A man or woman who not only gives love, but *draws* it—like an irresistible magnet. Throw such terms as *pleasant*, *agreeable*, *attractive*, *winsome*, *charming*, *generous*, and *giving* into the pot and you begin to capture the flavor.

The opposite? It's really not much of an alternative, is it? Who wants to be perceived as aloof, indifferent, insensitive, stingy, selfish, cold, and uncaring? For sure, no one enjoys living with such a person.

To become lovable is a tough pilgrimage. It's a long swim up river against the currents of our self-centered, sin-blasted nature. None of us are lovers by nature. God alone is love. But he shares recipes. That's what love does. This book is a recipe. I believe most of the ingredients are present to launch you on a different tack . . . a journey toward becoming more lovable.

I'm commanded to love you. It isn't always easy. I'm not mature enough to be able to love folks forever in spite of what they are. Do me a favor. Work on becoming more lovable. Make it easier for me to love you . . . *because* of what you are, not in spite of what you are. This book is designed to help you work on the "because of" dimension of love. No question about it . . . I am to love you in spite of what you are, but you are to love me because of what I am. In other words, I have the responsibility to make it as easy as possible for you to love me. If that's the case, I've become lovable.

More about that later.

Becoming lovable is not a mystery. There are some rather simple and logical steps to be taken. It's a process which begins in the inner landscape of the soul. The first half of this book wrestles with such issues as meaning, purpose, satisfaction, self-worth, and value. Scripture teaches that the heart will pursue what it values. You can develop your value. You can make yourself your own project instead of waiting for the other to change and meet your expectations. The transformation begins, then, with inside things, issues of the heart. There are decision points about God, ourselves, and others which must be confronted and made if we are to be liberated to become lovable.

Lovability is a gift you give yourself. God is the enabler, you are the recipient . . . if you choose to be. Admittedly, the tracks toward lovability are narrow. Conscience is God's gift to help us stay on track as we build momentum toward becoming more lovable. It keeps directing us back toward the only data base which liberates us to love and be loved.

But lovability is also one of the most precious gifts you can give to your loved ones. They, after all, are the ones who must share your name, your roof, your life. The second half of the book leaves behind the inside things and reveals how you can now transform your world. You can release loved ones from fear, build confidence, encourage healthy relationships, and convey truth which will transform their lives. Fresh insights on the nature of love provide specific stepping stones for the pilgrim serious about becoming more lovable. As you discover a new sense of your own value—value to God, yourself, and others—it will make a dramatic impact on the rest of your life.

PART ONE

TRANSFORMING YOURSELF: THE INSIDE STORY

C H A P T E R

1

DISCOVERING
A VALUABLE
PURPOSE

I'm forty-four years young. Good Lord willing, I've probably got another thirty to forty years left on my odometer. According to a thousand and one books, articles, booklets, and talk shows, I'm due for a mid-life crisis. When this "crisis" strikes, I'm apparently destined to ask some questions and do some crazy things. Questions like:

"Is the rat race worth it?"

"What's next?"

"Is this all there is?"

"I'm already halfway around in life; is this all the gusto I'll get?"

"If this is the good life, what's wrong?"

"What I've done with my life ... does it really count? Will it really make any difference in eternity?

Age old questions. Questions which haunt and taunt and tease.

The View from the Top

Can moving from a $75,000 house to a $150,000 home double happiness? Many secretly hope so. Is that what I need—what others really want? Perhaps a promotion, a raise, a career change, a different church, or a new mate will fill the growing crater called emptiness. If one tries a little harder, works a little longer, lives a little faster ... then perhaps satisfaction will surface. The temptation of life's fast lane calls some to leave the slow-laners behind, to join the jet set, to know the right people and be seen at the right places. Not a few wallow through the middle years, coasting toward retirement. It's all a race against the clock and the calendar.

But history haunts me. So many have set their course toward the American Dream. But is it just that, a dream? Does the riches-wealth-and-power option deliver? What happens to the person, the soul of the individual who enters the race for the pot at the end of the rainbow? Is the prize worth the price? Does the pursuit deliver? Does that kind of a commitment prove to be a wise course of action? What's it really like "at the top"?

Maybe satisfaction comes by being one of the financially secure ones, one of those who have position, power, and prestige. Lots of cars and condominiums, not to mention country club memberships.

Let's suppose you made it to the top, like ten of the world's most successful financiers who met at Chicago's Edgewater Beach Hotel in 1923. For the sake of illustration, you're number eleven. At this historic meeting, you find yourself rubbing shoulders with giants: the tycoons, the power brokers, those who have climbed the success ladder.

Looking around the exquisitely paneled boardroom you see the president of a large independent steel company, the president of the National City Bank, and the president of a large utility company. Next to him sits the distinguished president of a large gas company. Taking their places around the conference table are the president of the New York Stock Exchange, a great wheat speculator, a well-known leader in Wall Street, a member of the President's cabinet, the head of the world's largest monopoly, the president of the Bank of International Settlements . . . and you.

What a heady atmosphere! Casual conversation churns up yachts, exotic vacations, homes, estates, exclusive club memberships, and staggering financial transactions. You've moved on up! If a little bit is good, isn't more better, and the most best? These men had all found the pot at the end of the rainbow. In fact, they owned the rainbow! They didn't need to do any more searching for security or significance. They had it all, and then some.

What happened to these giants, these ten men who met at the top? Twenty-five years later:

> The president of the large independent steel company died bankrupt, having lived on borrowed money for the last five years of his life.

> The president of the great utility company died a fugitive from justice and penniless in a foreign land.

> The president of the large gas company went completely insane.

> The president of the New York Stock Exchange was released from Sing Sing Penitentiary.

> The member of the President's cabinet was pardoned so he could die at home.

> The great wheat speculator died abroad . . . insolvent.

> The great leader in Wall Street died . . . a suicide.

> The president of the Bank of International Settlements died . . . a suicide.

Like all of us, Ernest Hemingway sought security and significance. For him, literature was the roadmap—the track toward satisfaction. Hemingway's great passion was to be a successful writer. And he made it! As proof of his success he collected both the Pulitzer and Nobel prizes. His book *The Old Man and the Sea* made him wealthy and famous. He was free to do whatever his heart desired: buy whatever he wanted, travel wherever his whims directed. He sought excitement and adventure; was much married and divorced.

Apparently neither fame nor fortune satisfied. He came to his sunset years, and like countless others, added up his life, looked at the final figures, and concluded his quest was futile and not worth continuing. His suicide sent shock waves throughout the world.

Could it be that he really didn't fail? Could it be that he succeeded . . . in doing the wrong thing? He climbed the ladder of success. He reached the top! Was his ladder leaning against the wrong wall?

The Critical Question

Contrast Hemingway's wretched demise with the description of the last day of another wealthy man, perhaps the best-known historical figure in the world. His biographer tells us that:

> Abraham breathed his last and died in a ripe old
> age, an old man and satisfied with life.

I'm certain Abraham and Hemingway had lots in common. Both were wealthy. Both were well known. Both were perceived to be successful by their peers. But only Abraham died satisfied. He apparently found a different pot at the end of another rainbow.

I don't know about you, but when I come to the end of my life—whenever that may be—I'd like to look back over it and be satisfied.

Suppose *you* have forty years to live. If so, you are faced with an incredibly critical question. And I frankly believe this is *the* question that you—and I—must wrestle with now if we are going to finish our lives satisfied. The question is this: *When you come to the end of your life and have nothing but death to look forward to and nothing but memories to look back upon, what will you need to see to conclude that your life was a success and you are satisfied?*

I suspect we would jot down several items if we sat down to consider a "satisfaction list." Certainly "to love and be loved" would be near the top of most lists. Most of us long to be lovable. Most folks also want to be secure and significant.

It's tough, however, to pursue love for all we're worth if our lives are empty, evacuated of meaning and significance. Many suffer from the drifts, from destination sickness. "Pot collectors" abound. They flutter from rainbow to rainbow seeking gold that will satisfy. Abraham surveyed his life and concluded he was satisfied. I want to suggest that you are not ready to live those final forty years until you have determined what you will need to see at the end of your life to be satisfied.

Rich . . . but Shortsighted

In the twelfth chapter of his gospel, Luke recounts his Lord's description of a businessman who thought he had answered the satisfaction question. Mr. Businessman/Farmer was an agricultural tycoon. He belonged to the Million Dollar Round Table. Undoubtedly his Dun and Bradstreet rating was superb, his line of credit in six figures. A well-balanced financial portfolio adequately covered all the bases for the rest of his life. His pot was full!

But the Master Teacher describes the "mid-life crisis" which caught this wealthy entrepreneur by surprise . . . and unprepared. The agricultural business had treated him well. Because he had reaped bountifully, he anticipated a satisfying second half of life. "You've got it made!" the man told his soul. "Bank account's bursting, future's wired . . . and you're rolling in the chips. So relax. Enjoy. Prepare yourself for the 'good life.' You've worked hard, it's your turn." Didn't he deserve it? He had worked hard! It was time to cash in and turn on.

Almighty God, however, put his life on fast forward. There would be no second half. No time to build new barns. No time to contemplate a new chariot and a sun-splashed retirement. Eminently prepared to live, Mr. Farmer was unprepared to die.

And God called the man a fool.

Unexpectedly, in the midst of the night, a terrible pain rips through his chest. He cries out in pain and fear. A heart attack? Is this it? The end? It is. A sad voice rings out through the misty darkness settling over his soul, "You fool, this very night your soul is required of you."

Crossing into eternity, the once wealthy man is now poverty stricken. Naked, he is hastened to meet the God he ignored, the God who showered mercy upon him all his life.

He has an appointment with the One whose claims he refused to recognize, whose love he rejected, whose laws he ignored, whose paths he forsook.

He has nothing to say to a holy God. Nothing.

What would he give in exchange for his soul? A silo full of barley? A bank full of bucks? Good works? A promise to spend time with his neglected family? His tax deductible receipts? When life's tape runs out, there is no automatic reverse. It's over. *Finis.*

Restitution is impossible.

Reformation is not an option.

It's too late. The biblical warning is absolutely clear: "*It is appointed unto man once to die, and then judgment.*"

An instant before death, Mr. Successful Farmer (like his countless counterparts) was the envy of thousands, the companion of the high and mighty, a man who did many things well. Skillful management, hard work, and an intuitive feel for circumstances filled his barns to overflowing. Nothing wrong with that! Prudent investments expanded his enterprises, increased his capacities, and multiplied his profits . . . all for himself. Something is wrong with that.

With safe-deposit boxes brim full of gold, silver, precious stones, and stock certificates, Mr. Farmer had nothing to fear from future rainy days. He was well roofed. He'd thought of everything . . . almost.

Death was the one mid-life crisis he had not anticipated. When his local broker spoke, he listened, but the broker had no insight on the duration of his days. Had he known he'd passed mid-life years before, even his broker would have counseled him to consider a different set of priorities.

But it was too soon. Too soon to stop being self-centered. After all, one had to get ahead. Too soon to think about facing almighty God. Too soon to face up to the wrongs, the ugliness, the selfishness, and self-centeredness of his life. He'd hoped to do more for others, to become more lovable, to practice the Golden Rule more regularly, but now . . . it was too late. Too late to discover God's plan for his life, too late to discover the abundant life Jesus talked about. Too late to experience a spiritual birth into God's family . . . something his vast wealth and position couldn't purchase. He "gained the whole world," but lost his soul. He never found true significance or security. Driven by an insatiable need for more, he probably became less and less lovable as the years took their toll. Undoubtedly he had all the things he ever dreamed of having. He chose to get it all, have it all, and keep it all. He consistently turned down the opportunity to respond appropriately to his Creator.

Sometimes opportunity rejected is opportunity lost.

Although the barn-building farmer's life was cut short, his last day was likely a comfortable one. Probably dined on filet mignon and silky smooth chocolate mousse. Listened to some mellow music. And then that night . . . his last night . . . as he slipped between the cool satin sheets, it's possible he smiled contentedly over his achievements. His final thoughts before sleep we don't know. Might have been shallow, upbeat, profane. Could have been deep and searching. It's possible he had a momentary flare-up of heartburn . . . not the physical kind linked with Rolaids and Alka Seltzer. You know what I mean. He wondered if it was worth it all. Was he significant, was he secure? Did anyone really care about him, or was it his wealth they were after? If wealth was the key to security, maybe he wasn't rich enough. If position and power built significance, maybe he needed to climb higher. Perhaps he should take religion more seriously. If there's a payday someday, maybe he'd better get ready. His final thoughts? We can only guess.

One thing for sure, however. When the pleasing music died away, the next voice he heard wasn't pleasing at all. It was the voice of the Lord God, and it was full of sorrow.

"You fool."

And so he was.

Undoubtedly he'd heard that epithet . . . and worse . . . before. Goes with the territory. You can't climb the corporate ladder by always being Mr. Lovable C. Niceguy. Nice guys finish last! To get to the top you've got to push, crowd, control, and sometimes manipulate. Survival of the fittest is the name of the game. Getting there was the bottom line. Name-calling in the market place was simply part of the price one paid.

But when God calls a man a fool, he'd do well to listen.

A Destructive Pattern

An American newspaper editor described man as being "part of that strange race of people aptly described as spending their lives doing things they detest to make money they don't want to buy things they don't need to impress people they don't like." They detest, they don't want, they don't need, they don't like. Sounds like a race of unsatisfied, unlovable folks.

But most of us know that the self-seeking pattern is foolish even if we're unaware of Luke's commentary. Boredom, broken lives, desperate people, warped children, degraded passions, and sophisticated cruelty are easily seen once one scratches the veneer of respectability beneath which man hides. The masks are on parade, hiding status anxieties and bleeding ulcers. We've become accomplished fugitives from God, ourselves, and others.

T. S. Eliot observed that "we live in an age which is advancing progressively backwards." Interesting observation!

Backwards? I'm writing this manuscript on a sophisticated computer. Beats a pencil! What about modern science? Isn't technology an adequate messiah for man's dilemma?

History won't support such a hope. One searches the pages of scientific history in vain for any hint of help for man's soul, for the problems of meaning, of purpose. Certainly, diseases are being conquered so man can exist longer. But is prolonged existence without meaningful life a blessing? If life's pilgrimage is movement from the idealism and romanticism of youth to the cynicism and bitterness of old age, perhaps it's a blessing not to live so long. Living on the brink of nuclear disaster, even the taming of the atom is at best a questionable scientific achievement. Research indicates that modern psychology certainly isn't offering credible solutions to man's inner trauma.

How about you? When your life's clock runs down, what will help you conclude that you are satisfied with life? Money? Achievement? Ease? Community service? Church attendance? A nominal faith?

What will a holy God say about your life when you suddenly find yourself in his presence? Will it have been well spent? Will your life's purpose have been noble? Never mind the inevitable eulogy and the gracious comments by the coffin. Five seconds after you die, the only opinion that matters is your Creator's. His standard is perfection.

God called the affluent, barn-building businessman a fool. He had recognized no claim on his possessions. He had failed to discern the hand of God upon his life. He had made no provision for life after death. Apparently he believed material possessions and social position could bring satisfaction, significance, and security. Fact of the matter is, he lived and acted as though life revolved around him, as though he were God. Is it any wonder God questioned his wisdom? The Lord drove the point home with a piercing comment:

> This is how it will be with anyone who stores up
> things for himself but is not rich toward God.

The Possible Dream

Back up and think about the Lord's telling statement. Fools are men and women who are not rich toward God. Fools are rich toward themselves. "Who will get," the Lord asks, "what you have prepared for yourself?" Bad enough is the tragedy of a man who lives for himself, hoards for himself, and then discovers he goes naked into eternity. A tragedy of great magnitude. Not to be overlooked, however, is the tragedy of what happens to those significant others in this person's life. Nothing happens in isolation. Selfishness sends out poison ripples—waves that wash up their refuse and wreckage on other shores. You can't hide the

21

damage created by a self-centered life.

If he had not been a selfish (but no doubt respectable) fool, if he had been rich toward God, would the farmer have been satisfied with life? Could he have been rich toward God and also enjoyed his status, his position and power? It's possible. Rich-toward-God people *exchange their lives for what God has declared to be important*! Remember Abraham? Scripture reports that he "died in a ripe old age, an old man and *satisfied* with life" (Genesis 25:8 NASB). The ancient saint died with a smile on his face—he knew the secret of being rich toward God. Satisfaction is possible! Abraham made the exchange: his life for what God declared to be important. The farming fool didn't.

Only God's Word and people last forever. Focusing on God and people are the marks of a winner. Being rich toward God is the opposite of hoarding things for myself. It means saying no to me and yes to him. It often means saying no to me and yes to others. Life is such that if I "save" it, I lose it. If I lose it (give it away), I save it. Being "rich" involves abandoning all which is error, ungodly, ugly, and self-centered, and pursuing that which is right, honorable, and true.

The needs for security and significance sit like hungry puppies at the core of our being. Only the life built around truth has a ghost of a chance of satisfying their ravenous appetites. If the quest for significance does not travel on the tracks of truth, the longer one travels the more he becomes dissatisfied. It is virtually impossible to build significance into people and ignore truth. It is impossible to become lovable and ignore truth. It is impossible to be a caring, loving individual and ignore truth. Thus the rich-toward-God person has exchanged his life for God's Word (truth) and people. The result? Satisfaction. The result? We become more lovable! There is no plan B. Is it any wonder the Lord declared, "I am the way and the truth and the life"? (John 14:6). It's significant to realize that Abraham wasn't the only one satisfied with his life. God was satisfied with Abraham's life, too! When the end came, God did not call him a fool. He wasn't. *Life isn't worth living if Abraham's experi-*

ence is not an option for us today. The alternative? Achievement without satisfaction. A gradual drift away from people and relationships. Meaninglessness, emptiness, futility; gradual loss of vitality, health, and strength; and then death and judgment.

Was Abraham better than the wealthy farmer? No. Did he try harder? Probably not. Did he earn God's favor by being religious, by keeping the Golden Rule, by putting lots of bucks in the offering plate? No. Abraham, like the farmer, violated God's laws. Both were sinners. Abraham lied, deceived, and at times questioned God's promises. He was not a religious crackpot or a goody-two-shoes. He simply believed God.

The fact is, Abraham was fabulously wealthy. He probably could have bought out the foolish farmer several times over and still had enough left for the IRS. He was crawling with servants. Had so much livestock it was tough to keep track of them. Everyone knew he was rich . . . even his servants. They bragged about it:

> "The LORD has blessed my master abundantly, and he has become wealthy. He has given him sheep and cattle, silver and gold, menservants and maidservants, and camels and donkeys" (Genesis 24:35).

Genesis 13:2 records that Abraham "had become very wealthy in livestock and in silver and gold." Wealth was not the issue. It was God, after all, who had made him wealthy. Because God was central to Abraham's life, even his wealth didn't keep him from being satisfied!

So how does one live and die satisfied? By choosing to be rich toward God. By moving from self-centeredness to God-centeredness. Only then can I break out of the prison of self and give myself away to others. As I do that, I become more lovable.

C H A P T E R

2

DISCERNING YOUR ULTIMATE VALUE

"**W**hat's the coin worth?" I don't know, but someone does. Someone also knows the value of your stamps, antiques, and prized porcelains.

"What's the car worth?"

Give me its year, model, miles, and accessories, and a quick check with a blue book will provide the answer.

By the way, *what are you worth*? Does it depend upon whom I talk to . . . or is there a more objective standard?

Perhaps your husband treats you like junk. And maybe he feels like junk. Mr. and Mrs. Junk. Is your value, then, dependent upon the junkman's subjective appraisal? Can you become lovable if you perceive yourself as worthless? Would you act and feel different if someone perceived you to be a great treasure?

I suspect that you would. Our sense of worth is greatly influenced by what we see of ourselves reflected in the faces of others. It's as though we come into life carrying a bucket in each hand. Emblazoned on one bucket is a big plus sign (+). Into this bucket go all the positive bits of information we receive about ourselves. The other bucket bears a big minus sign (—); it holds the negatives: the put-downs, the sarcastic remarks, the cruel and insensitive comments which focus on our weaknesses and inadequacies. It's hard to be lovable if we don't feel loved.

If the negative is not balanced—indeed overweighed—by an overwhelming bucket of positives, our personal sense of worth, our self image, is in danger of becoming warped and distorted. Sometimes we become so buried under negatives that we put a lid on the positive bucket and are no longer capable of receiving and accepting a genuinely positive compliment.

There is an old Yiddish proverb that says, "If one man calleth thee a donkey, pay him no mind. If two men call thee a donkey, get thee a saddle." Maybe that's good advice. But then again, what if you're acting and thinking and feeling like a donkey when in reality you are the son or daughter of the King of kings? Donkeys can be very lovable creatures. People who feel like donkeys find it more difficult to feel lovable.

A Sin Against Eagles

Ron Ritchie, a friend of mine from seminary days, once asked me if I'd ever seen an eagle in a cage. "Yes," I replied. His response? "You're wrong. If it was in a cage, it wasn't an eagle." Eagles belong to the sky, not the cage or the barnyard. Labeling an eagle a chicken doesn't make it a chicken—even if it lives in a chicken coop, crows on a fencepost, and pecks at table scraps in the barnyard!

Chicken-coop eagles are tragic! By assuming a chicken identity, the king of birds forfeits the sky, the far horizons, and a wind-swept nest that crowns a mountain.

Even more pathetic, however, is a person who would stoop to treating an eagle like a chicken. Jonathan Edwards understood this travesty when he wrote:

> The ultimate good is to treat something according to its true value.

Eagles must be treated like eagles. Not to treat an eagle like an eagle, then, would be the ultimate sin against eagledom. Certainly a truly lovable person would treat eagles like eagles!

Eagles who perceive themselves as chickens will think, act, and respond like chickens (and probably treat fellow eagles like barnyard fowl as well). Folks who perceive themselves to be donkeys will line up to be saddled. In large measure, you become what you think you are—even if your perceptions are distorted. If you think you have no value, that you can never be lovable, then for all *practical* purposes . . . you're probably right!

If I'm treated like junk, I feel like junk. If I feel like junk, I act like junk. If I act like junk, I'm treated like junk; if I'm treated like junk . . . and so it goes.

If the ultimate good is for you to be treated according to your true value, then it is of critical importance for both you and me to understand that fact and to respond appropriately. Notice that I said both of us. If Jonathan Edwards is right, the ultimate good is for you to respond appropriately to your own true value. And it will certainly make it easier for me to love you if you are resting secure in that value.

Give Us a Break

But isn't *agape* love something that's unconditional? Am I not to love "in spite" of your inadequacies and imperfections? The resounding answer is yes!

Not many, however, can sustain this kind of "tough love" over long periods of time. Warmth, affection, friendship, and companionship are fruits of two-way love and are not possible in a one-way love relationship. Many healthy relationships begin with tough love, that is, they are one-sided. One person is doing the initiating, giving, and sacrificing. This is the basic idea contained in what is often called "agape" love. Without it, many relationships would never get off the ground. Usually it is the beginning point of love, it is a set of actions which overcomes, which breaks down the self-centeredness of another. The goal, however, is *phileo*, the warm affection of mutual admiration and appreciation.

We expect infants to be self-centered. We love them, care for them, protect them in spite of their selfish demands. If you're big enough to read this, however, it is neither right nor fair for you to continue to receive the faithful love of another and remain in protracted infancy. At some point, love should become reciprocal. "We love Him because He first loved us."

At just this point, however, many Christians cop out. Their rationalization goes something like this: "A*gape* love means to love in spite of what I am. You're supposed to love me *unconditionally*, therefore I won't (and have no obligation to) change." So they wait like bullfrogs on the lily pads of life for that prince, that perfect lady or gentlemen to come and love them . . . warts and all . . . forever.

So what's the point? Give me a break! H*elp me to love you*. And give your marriage partner, your associates, and your relatives a break. We want to love you. We haltingly depend on God to help us love you. But let's face it, sometimes you (and all of us) aren't easy to love. We're not too lovable!

How do you give us a break? By becoming more lovable. And how is that accomplished? By wrestling with this issue called "value." The highway toward lovability is paved with the stones of value. No other pavement delivers. Becoming more valuable is a major part of the solution.

Value and Lovability

Matthew 6:19-34 teaches us that *if we expect the care, the attention, and the love of another, we must pay careful attention to value.* The crucial, foundational step toward lovability is to understand the dynamics of value and its magnetic influence on the heart. Value tugs at the heart. Matthew 6 helps us understand some of the dynamic relationships between value and lovability.

First, *the heart pursues value.* "For where your treasure is, there your heart will be also" (Matthew 6:21). The affections camp close to treasure. Tell me what a person values, and I will show you the location of his heart. We get turned on over that which is valuable to us. When we say, "his heart just isn't in it," we are referring to apathetic, unenthusiastic behavior.

When a man's heart isn't in his marriage, for example, it means he no longer perceives value in the relationship. The tug is gone. Notice that I did not say there was no longer value in it. He has simply ceased to look for it. He doesn't see it. Recognition (or lack of it), however, does not determine reality.

Admittedly, much of the original value in a relationship may be difficult to see. A gracious-spirited wife has become a nagging, whining woman. It happens. A once trim, handsome gentleman has become a sloppy, overweight, demanding social boor. That happens, too! People change. In the face of such value-diminishing changes, love slips out the back door to pursue another value, to seek other treasure. When the precious becomes profane, hearts do an about-face.

Second, *the heart provides for what it values*. Put yet another way, there is a direct relationship between value and provision of need. Christ reminds us that the God who feeds the birds and clothes the flowers will surely take care of you. Why? "Are you not much more valuable than they?" (Matthew 6:26). The answer, my friend, is yes, and the issue is value.

Look again at the phrase in the heart of that verse. "Much more." Has a ring to it, doesn't it? M*uch more*! He's talking about you. Is the picture coming into focus? His heart not only follows what he values, he provides for what is precious to him. Therefore, don't worry about tomorrow . . .

We understand this principle. If the garage-mate of your tired Toyota is a new Turbo 928, it is quite possible that the new toy will get better care. We tend to focus our resources, our time, our affection, and our energy on what we value.

Unfortunately (you knew it was coming), we are often blind to *true* value. We miss it. Sin has warped, distorted, and redirected our hearts into self-centered paths. Suffering from dislocated hearts, we make terrible investments. It's not unusual for us to invest heavily in that which proves to be of no value, or—worse yet—we invest nothing in that which is priceless. Whatever the nature of our investments—good or bad—we pour our lives into what we perceive to be valuable.

Third, *the heart pays attention to what it values*. No question about it. Who doesn't want and need attention? Even big folks do, though they often deny it. It is a simple fact that we give our undivided attention to that which we count valuable. Ask any football widow or hunter's wife or bridge player's husband. As a general rule, the more valuable we perceive something to be, the more attention it receives. We want, for instance, to be with people we value. The others we usually (and unfortunately) ignore.

Fourth, *the heart protects what it values*. Again and again our Lord tells us not to worry. Assured that we are much more valuable than his birds, we are encouraged to rest secure and anxiety-free. He will meet the needs of our tomorrows. And we have good reason to rest secure, because his perfect and unchanging character assures an appropriate response to our value.

In a nutshell, then, *to become more lovable, we must become more valuable*. Like an Indian trailing a deer, the heart follows value. It lives next door to its treasure. Lovable people find their way into others' treasure chests . . . and make every effort to stay there!

Why Lovability Languishes

Why do we find love slipping away from our relationships? Why do we sometimes feel like last year's model? Why do we find ourselves overlooking the precious value of others? Could it be that our own self-centeredness has distorted our perception of true value? Perhaps our own fingerprints have smudged the lenses. Perhaps *we* have lost some value in the sight of others. We've slipped, we've changed, we've become negligent, forgetful, and unappreciative. Our "loved ones" . . . have found new loves.

Why? Why do we abandon that which was previously valued and neglect that which has obvious value? Certainly one reason is that whatever we value is ultimately that which in some way meets a need. A bus company captured this truth in an ad campaign not long ago. The ad caption read:

DISCERNING YOUR ULTIMATE VALUE

When You Deal in Basic Needs,
You're Always Needed.

Why are you needed? Because you meet basic needs. We all need love, security, acceptance, esteem, significance, and beauty. We need meaningful and intimate fellowship. We need to know and be known. We need to be needed, to belong. God himself said, "It is not good for man to be alone."

But what happens? We make a contribution to family needs, we cook meals, clean house, bring home the bacon, sacrifice our time for others, drive carpools, go to soccer games, and yet . . . feel used and unappreciated. What has gone wrong, what is so obviously missing that we exploit and are exploited, that we care and are crushed, that we give and are taken? Why do we find ourselves becoming less lovable and less valuable?

There are at least three ways in which we become less lovable. One sure method of losing lovability is to devalue others—to fail to respond appropriately to their value. If I treat you like yesterday's newspaper, if I put you down, it becomes increasingly difficult for you to perceive me as a caring, lovable person. My lovability decreases if I am unloving toward you. I've lost my tug! Criticism, nagging, aloofness, and indifference are potent "tug killers."

We may also find ourselves losing our tug when others devalue us. Unless we maintain a firm, biblical grasp on who we really are in Jesus Christ, such insensitive devaluation may eat away at the underpinnings of our personality. That's a nice way of saying if we don't understand our true value, we're apt to get the slats kicked out of us. We can become defensive, withdrawn—even emotionally crippled. When others call us donkeys, we line up to be saddled. It's difficult to be up on someone else if we're down on ourselves.

In order to survive such inappropriate treatment with our lovability intact, we must temper the careless, cruel comments of others with a steady diet of what *God* has to say about us. Jesus Christ did not die for donkeys. King's kids must not perceive themselves as beasts of burden!

Finally, we become less lovable when we devalue our-selves through default. Through carelessness and neglect, it is possible to stop growing. We become sloppy, critical, demanding . . . pushy. Neglect of basic grooming and personal hygiene coupled with a deteriorating, pessimistic, critical attitude usually succeeds in bleaching out whatever lovability remains. Under such circumstances, hearts go AWOL.

So how do you become more lovable? By *becoming more valuable*. How valuable are you . . . as a friend . . . as a companion . . . as a growing, stretching, positive, contributing, affirming person? Successful people are people who find out how the system works and then get on the good side of how things work. Lovable people are perceived as valuable people. That's how the system works.

So get on the good side of how things work. Think value. *Value* value. Tug, tug, tug! The major challenge? We've lost our tug.

Where Devaluation Begins

Why do you and I find ourselves investing in junk—and bypassing treasure? It's almost as though someone crept in behind our backs and changed all the price tags. Rat poison is being sold as bread—treasures are being discounted, wholesaled, and peddled as cheap trinkets. Why?

Someone really did change the price tags. Something did happen. Something catastrophic. Man lost his dignity. And even though this process of devaluation began in the Garden of Eden, it did not begin with the devaluation of man.

It began with an attempted devaluation of God.

It began when man succumbed to a blatant attack upon the character of God.

"Come on, Eve!" said the tempter. "God's got you on a short leash. He doesn't really care for you. If he did, he wouldn't restrict you! He knows that if you eat fruit from this tree, you will be like God. So you see? He's selfish. He doesn't want you to have the very best. Besides . . . he didn't really mean what he said."

Satan is oh-so-slippery. The one thing he *didn't* want, in spite of his accusation, was for man to be like God. Nor did he want man to conceive of himself as a creature, dependent and accountable to an infinite, holy Creator. The devil's desire has always been to focus man's attention downward, not upward. Central to his purpose and program is the *redefinition of man*. There is a large pasture near our home which is often full of people. I call them the "mushroom people." Whether walking or on hands and knees, they share one thing in common . . . they are always looking down. Down toward the grass, leaves, and dirt. Down toward the shadowy habitat of the mushroom. That's what they want. They'll spend hours searching for the right mushroom: the one which is capable of giving them some kind of a high. Scratching like hens in barnyard dirt, they have no thought of "mounting up with wings as eagles." They've built their life, their hope, around a fundamental error.

Israel committed the same error. They literally put God "out to pasture." Listen to the psalmist's words: "At Horeb they made a calf and worshiped an idol cast from metal." The result? Read it carefully. "*They exchanged their Glory for an image of a bull, who eats grass.*" Change the bull to an ape, and we've arrived in the twentieth century. Are you simply the product of time plus energy plus chance? The naked ape? A cosmic orphan? For what are we exchanging our Glory?

Definition is fundamental to responsible, appropriate living. "Who am I?" is life's most foundational question. "What do I do?"—the question of responsibility—must wait until the question of identity is settled.

Romans chapter 1 picks up Satan's subtle process of devaluation through redefinition. And here is the apostle Paul's big idea: *Interpersonal devaluation can always be traced back to a devaluation of God*. The attempt to change or alter one's understanding of the Creator's being is the first step in demeaning the value of man, the creature. Listen to Paul's words:

> For although they knew God, they neither glorified him as God nor gave thanks to him, but

their thinking became futile and their foolish hearts were darkened. Although they claimed to wise, they became fools *and exchanged the glory of the immortal God for images made to look like mortal man and birds and animals and reptiles* (Romans 1:21-23, italics mine).

What Price Diamonds?

Although Romans 1 records man's attempt to change and modify his concept of God, this "redefinition" is an exercise in futility. God is changeless—not subject to the fickle imaginations of men. It shouldn't surprise us that man attempts to alter the image of a holy and righteous God. If I don't intend to live within the boundary conditions of God's holy character, I need to alter his image enough so that I can live with my unrighteousness. Nevertheless, man's refusal to respond responsibly to the revelation of God's character does not alter in the slightest degree the reality of God's holy Self. Acceptance, however, of a distorted, warped, man-made view of ultimate reality (God or whatever) has tragic consequences for man. He may wish to will a holy God out of existence. His wish will not be realized. Instead, he will take his place before the throne of the Almighty and be measured by the standard of divine perfection.

The reality of God's character is in no way influenced by the beliefs of man. It is objective, unchanging.

All true value, except God himself, has *derived* value. It is valuable because it can be traced back to God. It is "because of" value. In contrast to this, God *is* value. His holy nature and character forms the foundation, the boundary conditions of all true value. Everything which does not share his essence has a contingent, temporary, or utilitarian value. In other words, it is valuable so long as it is useful and continues to meet a need.

For example, it is entirely possible (but not probable) that diamonds could become worthless. For some reason man has decided they are of great value, and he will do almost anything to get them. "Diamonds," so the folklore goes, "are a girl's best friend." But there is nothing intrinsic to a diamond which demands it to be valuable.

A diamond, after all, is just a rock. There is no moral imperative or necessity which compels me to treasure them. There is no Eleventh Commandment which says, "Thou shalt value diamonds." Their value is subjective. I can choose not to value them. I can ignore them altogether and not sin by doing so. And if enough people chose not to value diamonds, they could become worthless.

If, however, everyone chose not to value God, or attempted to "redefine" him, it would not change his character one iota! His is not a derived value, subject to the whims of the marketplace. Again, He *is* value, no matter what earthly philosophy happens to be in vogue.

God's Blue Book

But what, you might ask, does all this discussion have to do with my value and lovability?

Simply this: If your friend, husband, wife, parent, or child perceives God to be of no relevance or value, *you* will suffer the consequences. Here's the principle. *As one is toward God, so is he in all other relationships.*

Remember the diamonds—treatment is directly related to perception of value. Redefine man as something other than a created being, and he becomes profane, a cosmic accident, the apex of an arbitrary evolutionary process. Label him an animal, a grass-eating ox. As such, he is subject to being herded, exploited, and manipulated. An eagle has been caged . . . a human has been devalued.

Unlike diamonds, however, man's true value is not subjective. It is not based on what I, you, or someone else might think or imagine. If the whole world, as a matter of fact, decided you were worthless, it would not change your essential value. Why? *Because as a believer, you share both the image and nature of the unchanging God himself.* Peter reminds us that we have become "partakers of the divine nature." Your value is tied to Christ. He is the magnetic north pole of your essential worth. The Almighty God is the infinite reference point, the ultimate standard, the "cosmic blue book" of your value. He created you in his image and like-ness. Your value was written in blood at the cross. And whatever God values is valuable. In a cosmic sense, no other opinion matters.

Remember our Lord's word? "Are you [that's *you*, my friend] not much more valuable than they?" The answer is *yes*. Whether you—or anyone else—recognize it or not.

The "Baby Fae" case of the mid-1980s brought some of these issues into the headlines. The tiny infant needed a new heart. No donor was available, and death was immi-nent. In desperation, her physicians transplanted the heart of a baboon into her chest. It seemed her only chance at that time. Some of us were startled when animal rights ac-tivists protested on behalf of the sacrificed baboon. Did there have to be two deaths, they questioned? Were not the two deaths equally tragic? They were not! When God de-clared that man was made in his image and likeness, he put an impassable, uncrossable gulf between the animal and human kingdoms. Modern man has exchanged his glory for an ape . . . a baboon, if you will. Mankind is sacred. Magnificent as they are, animals are not sacred. They do not share the nature of God.

Why Man Devalues God

But why has man exchanged his glory for a grass-eating ox? Why does he tamper with the definition of the revealed God of nature and holy Scripture? As suggested earlier, from God's unchanging character flow all the moral im-peratives which obligate men to live according to divine standards. The ultimate rule book of life is a direct out-growth of God's nature—just as most family rules are a re-flection of the character of the parents. If I alter my concept of God, the forbidding Ten Commandments can more eas-ily be watered down to "Ten Suggestions," enabling me to continue a godless life style with less guilt.

Sinful man is not comfortable being reminded that a holy and righteous God is the ultimate reality. Choosing a degraded, devalued concept of God, however, has an inter-esting side effect. Man becomes like what he worships. His worship shapes his very life. Note carefully the words of the psalmist:

> The idols of the nations are silver and gold,
>> made by the hands of men.
> They have mouths, but cannot speak,
>> eyes, but they cannot see;
> they have ears, but cannot hear,
>> nor is there breath in their mouths.
> *Those who make them will be like them,*
>> *and so will all who trust in them.*
>>>> (Psalm 135:15-18, italics mine).

The Greeks and Romans produced gods who were both sensuous and promiscuous. These "deities" were swingers in the fullest sense of the word. Dancing around Mount Olympus, they indulged in every pleasure. Becoming like the gods they worshiped, the Greeks and Romans enshrined temple prostitution as their favorite form of "religion." In the name of their gods, women suffered the devaluation of sexual abuse. In the name of religion, men acted like animals—and worse.

A Terrible Exchange

Paul goes on to illustrate the fact that our character is cast in the mold of our concentration. Once man chooses an inappropriate response to God, his treatment of his fellow man becomes equally inappropriate.

Note what happens. After refusing to glorify God, man "exchanged the truth of God for a lie, and worshiped and served created things rather than the Creator" (Romans 1:25). The result: sexual impurity (v. 24), shameful lusts and perversions (v. 26), and every kind of depravity.

Paul highlights the devastating effects of viewing Almighty God as a "golden calf" or some other creature. Devalued and stripped of his glory, man's foolish mind becomes darkened. Paul says he can't even *think* right anymore. He can no longer perceive true value. As a result, people become objects to be used and abandoned. People are viewed as bearers of function rather than beings. So viewed, wives feel like maids, mothers, and mistresses. Others are "valued" as long as they contribute to the individual's self-centered interests and desires. "I love you . . . if" becomes the byword of this self-centered crowd.

From the very moment a man exchanges the untainted glory of God for something tainted and corruptible, two things happen: First, he defines (devalues) the nature of man; second, he acts accordingly. When man casts God in bronze or gold and worships the "Golden Calf," the product of his imagination, everything changes. "God? Oh, he's out in the pasture somewhere chewing his cud. We don't pay any attention to him." He's a "safe" god, a god with fangs and claws removed.

When God is put out to pasture, all hell breaks loose. As long as we view ourselves as evolution's children, anything goes. We're free as the birds and beasts. Assigned animal value, man lines up to be saddled.

And we *are* saddled. Saddled with epidemic divorce, increasing perversion, multiplying abortions, and unchecked sexual immorality. We have been devalued and debased. Major trends in contemporary art and music herald man's descent into despair and depravity. Our divine umbilical cord unplugged, we have settled for the lowest common denominator. Human value is no longer tied to an infinite, divine, holy being. It floats and fluctuates on the current tide of public opinion. Morality is purely statistical. It is no longer viewed as the reflection of the character of Almighty God. Consequently, if the unborn child (an image bearer of God himself) is an inconvenience, kill it. If the wife becomes a bore, bail out. If kids become a liability, leave. And so we kill, bail out, and leave.

The Poison and the Antidote

Two things feed this poisoned, degraded view of other people. First, sin which expresses itself as self-centeredness. This perspective automatically predisposes us to devalue, exploit, and manipulate others. Second, the devaluation of God flattens any moral fences, enlarges our comfort zone, and encourages us to indulge our self-centeredness.

What, then, is the antidote to this cruel distortion of human dignity? It begins with a return to reality about God. *The single most important fact about you is what comes to your mind when you think about God.* Don't hurry past that fact . . . it's true. We are able to perceive, to think rightly about the particulars of everyday life only when we think accurately about him. A child becomes ill. If you perceive God to be a resident policeman, you may feel that your child's illness is divine punishment. If God is thought to be a doting, almost senile grandfather, you may conclude you can "get away with murder."

Solomon was right. Nothing less than the fear of God is the beginning of wisdom. A*nd responding appropriately to him demands that I respond appropriately to his workmanship.* That's you. I must never profane what he has made sacred, for the God who created man and woman observed his craftsmanship and declared, "It is *very good.*"

The second phase in recovering from the loss of dignity is a return to realty about yourself. You are not a donkey, a chicken, or a grass-eating ox. A sinner, yes. Fallen, yes . . . but not junk. Redeemed, true . . . but not cheaply. It was precious blood spilled to restore your dignity and reaffirm your value. The eighth psalm reminds us that we were "created a little lower than God, and crowned with glory and honor." Let's reaffirm the concept: The ultimate good for you is to treat yourself according to your true value.

To paraphrase that Yiddish proverb: "If man calleth thee a grass-eating ox, pay him no mind. If God calleth thee his child, put on thy royal robes!" Tied by creation to God, divine pedigrees and royal robes replace bananas, naked apes, and grass-eating oxen. Thumb through the Bible for your definition. It alone holds the key to the recovery of your dignity. Open your closet door and peek at those royal robes. May as well wear them; they won't fit anyone else.

Third, treat others according to their true value. That wife, that husband, parent, child, or friend feels put out to pasture, relegated to the barn, harnessed for the use of others. So go for a treasure hunt in a nearby pasture. Treat those discouraged ones with dignity and affirm their value and worth. Do whatever is necessary to make them feel special, wanted, and valuable. Remember . . . not to treat them according to their true value is the ultimate . . . evil.

Like a metal detector, the heart feels the tug of value. It is an incurable treasure hunter, created by God to pursue value. When you and I affirm the value *of* others, we confirm our value *to* others. People like to be valued! In other words, as we affirm, our value is reaffirmed . . . and we become more lovable.

C H A P T E R

3

DEVELOPING YOUR PRACTICAL VALUE

Yes, we do have permanent, eternal, objective value because of our relationship with the Creator. It's as real as tomorrow's sunrise, and no one can take it away from you.

But that's only part of the story!

We are indeed "much more valuable than the birds," and it's certainly true that in the final analysis, only God's unchanging value judgment matters.

But don't stop there!

A long road stretches before you—a bright, inviting trail that winds ahead into the distance. The pathway to value and lovability begins with discovering your God-given, unchangeable worth. Now . . . enter into the journey. For the rest of your days, you may choose to follow that path and *develop* your value—growing in love and lovability with each passing year.

Don't short circuit God's master plan. Don't pull the plug on an eternal symphony. Don't shut the book when you've only turned the first page. The quest begins . . . right now.

Intrinsic Value

We who are self-centered can become other-centered, we who are indifferent can become caring, we who are selfish can become generous, we who are valued little can become much valued. It is important that we distinguish between our objective, unchanging value and our subjective, changing value.

Intrinsic value is the value we have as creatures who share the image of our divine Creator. Both creature and Creator are thinking, feeling, acting beings. Our essential being reflects his being. And this Creator of ours loved us sinners to the point of actually becoming man and dying on our behalf so that through redemption (the new birth), we could be restored to original specifications. Christ's sacrificial death, based on his love for us, is a great assurance of our value. As Ethel Waters put it, "Honey, God don't sponsor no flops."

But despite our role as image-bearers of God, all is not well. With the fall of man came qualities and characteristics of negative value. We have inherited and cultivated habits and responses which irritate and tear down rather than build. In a nutshell, we've "blown the blueprint." The evidence is all around us.

Marriage quickly surfaces these inadequacies. We find that we must live with each other as marred, inadequate, and at times offensive beings. As the dream world of courtship dissolves into the daily realities of marriage, our focus shifts from the ideal to the real, from essence to experience, from theory to practice. The inevitable reappraisal often feeds the fires of disillusionment and devaluation. That Cadillac we married turns out to be a Ford with two flat tires. And by the way, *your* cover is blown, too. You're not the Mercedes your partner anticipated, either. So you start kicking each other's hubcaps and denting each other's fenders. Your mate must never be allowed to forget that he or she is only a Ford—with a stick shift and blackwall tires.

Reminding the other of his or her "Fordishness" is a protective measure, designed to prop up a sagging sense of personal value. But discrediting our partner is a form of devaluation. Such a response usually overlooks value and certainly kills the incentive to develop or increase in value. Why should I act like a Cadillac if I'm treated like a Ford?

Thankfully, our God doesn't treat us like Fords. Through redemption he rescues people from the wrecking yards of life and offers them potential far beyond their greatest expectations. "If anyone is in Christ [a Christian], he is a new creation; the old has gone, the new has come!" (2 Corinthians 5:17). God stamps "paid in full" across the accounts of his children, and posts no trespassing signs across the garbage dumps of their past. Through gates of splendor his kids will walk . . . all because of Calvary.

Practical Value

In addition to our objective, unchanging, intrinsic worth, we have several subjective, changing values which we can either increase or decrease. The first of these is the utilitarian or practical value whose presence contributes so much to our lovability. Part of our worth is the skills, abilities, and special aptitudes which we exhibit and others observe and appreciate. The old saying, "The way to a man's heart is through his stomach" isn't a bad illustration of this point. Cooking skills *are* a valuable asset. So are good housekeeping skills. A hard-working, diligent bread-winner has great value and worth.

Faithfulness in the routine, the unpleasant, often unseen things is an important indication of value. Toilets get clogged, floors need mopping, lawns need mowing, houses must be painted, meal preparation never ends, the sick must be cared for, bills demand regular, systematic attention. A well-run house is a victory, not an accident.

Granted, not all are equally proficient in the kitchen or marketplace. In spite of the fact that practical value varies from person to person, we all have the potential of growing in our practical value to others. We must continually remind ourselves that God has uniquely gifted each of us with capacities and practical abilities which have the potential of adding richness and beauty to the lives of others.

Do you want to know an excellent way to add practical value to your lovability level? *Take the importance of little things seriously*! Things like a simple note, a pretty card, a surprise bouquet, an opened door, a kind word, a helping hand, a touch, a listening ear. Friend, that list is loaded with tug power. Who can place a premium on these things? Even the simplest of them may come to hold a cherished place in the memory of another. An act backed by a caring attitude helps the practical become precious. A habit of helping is one compelling way to build value and become more lovable.

Aesthetic Value

God has built into man a deep appreciation for beauty. The ability to perceive, produce, and respond to beauty is a God-given capacity. He does, and so do we as his creation. Mountains, trees, and pristine lakes leave me in awe. Something within me wants to applaud the beauty of a sunset, a symphony, and the stellar splendor of a clear summer night. An authentic, carefully prepared Italian dinner receives my enthusiastic plaudits as well, but in my humble estimation, nothing is more beautiful than a beautiful woman. Nothing. Most of us men tend to fall in love with the package and not the contents. Yet *both* package and contents are critically important. Beauty really tugs!

There is no denying, however, that gravity eventually wins the battle. We bulge, wrinkle, and some go bald. *There is, however, an appropriate physical condition for each age level*. To become sloppy in physical appearance, dress, and personal hygiene decreases your aesthetic value. Such a pattern reduces the tug. This is especially true if friends and loved ones place considerable value on personal appearance.

Not to care is probably the biggest error. Almost everyone has some part that is too big, too little, too thin, or too fat. Some inherited their problem. Others created it. Some physical problems are solvable, many are not. Gluttony and lack of discipline contribute substantially to physical deterioration. Poor health habits, insecurity, bitterness, and regret also encourage physical neglect. As someone put it, our body and souls are so closely linked together they catch each other's diseases.

For sake of illustration, let's assume that staying in shape, dressing carefully, and eating properly are important to you. Ten years ago you married the quarterback on the football team. At that time he was full of tug! You've continued to take personal pride in your appearance. The cheerleading outfit still fits. Hubby can't come close to buttoning his letterman's jacket. Pants don't fit. He comes home from work, changes into jeans and an undershirt, and sits passively in front of the TV—except at mealtimes. The carefully prepared meal disappears in a flash and it's back to the tube again. The major challenge of your evening is to see that the chip and dip is replenished at commercial times.

So he burps and groans his way through another evening and then hits the sack. Exciting! The situation is often reversed. The well-dressed, healthy businessman brings home a client to meet his sloppy, unkempt wife. In either case, respect and value can be greatly diminished by physical neglect.

Want to become more lovable? The heart pursues what it values. Therefore, do what is appropriate to be as attractive as possible. Demonstrate care and concern for hygiene and personal appearance. If you don't, nobody else will. If you do, it may make someone's heart feel the tug.

By far the most important dimension of your aesthetic value, however, is spiritual, not physical. We all know people who are striking in their physical appearance and yet are anything but beautiful. We also know some rather ordinary-looking people who bubble with beauty.

I have yet to meet a man who courted, pursued, and wooed a complaining, critical, negative, nagging woman. But I know lots of men who are married to such creatures. By the same token, no woman in her right mind is attracted to an aloof, indifferent, uncaring man—yet countless husbands now fit that precise description.

Have these men and women lost value in the eyes of friends and family? *You'd better believe it!* Are they harder to love? No question about it. The apostle Peter counseled women that the best way to leverage their husbands toward maturity was to take seriously the principle of inner beauty (1 Peter 3). God himself is said to value the adornment of a meek and quiet spirit.

What's the flavor of your spirit? Sweet or sour? Negative or positive? Caring or caustic? Constructive or destructive?

Here's a major clue to the cosmetics of your spirit: Check the tone of your voice when you speak. Are you in a correcting mode? Eliminate the scold, the contempt, the complaint, the whine. Keep in mind that thirty-eight percent of communication is tone of voice!

The goal, inner beauty, is produced by the Spirit of God as his nature works through those who have become his children. Ultimately, beauty is the possession and expression of God's nature. All true Christians possess the nature of God through the new birth. But by no stretch of the imagination do all believers *express* God's nature. Many claim truth and produce ugliness. A beautiful spirit is one that is in tune with God's Spirit, one which is walking in daily fellowship with him. We *cannot* be caring and loving toward one another and indifferent toward God.

Potential Value

Potential value is yet another key to becoming lovable. All have it. Some develop it. This value grows in tug power as a result of growth, development, and learning. When we consider potential value, we are talking about the very essence of the abundant life. As someone has well said, "when we cease to learn, we cease to live." Tragically, many die at age twenty and are buried at sixty-five! When you throw in the towel, you're harder to love . . . especially if your mate hasn't.

The Lord nourishes and cherishes his bride, the Church, so that it will grow. He doesn't want us to remain infants—in any area of our lives. Love nourishes. Why? So that the object of love will grow. If you love me, you desire to invest in my growth and development. Love encourages its object to reach, stretch, risk, and grow. How? By talking about it? No, by reaching, stretching, risking, and growing! If I really love someone else, my own personal growth must be a high-agenda item.

Picture, if you will, a husband who reads voraciously,

attends seminars and conferences, and is continually working with a hobby or new area of interest. His wife? She died years ago, although she continues to keep house, fix meals, and wash clothes.

Does this wife have utilitarian value? Yes. Potential for becoming more valuable, and hence more lovable? Absolutely. The issue is not so much available time as it is mindset and direction.

It may be that hubby refuses to let his wife grow. Threatened by her potential achievement, he attempts to keep her domesticated and dumb. In so doing, he devalues her and she become less valuable to him. They both lose. Personality, a product of relationship, can be warped by such a domineering, threatened, insecure person.

The point? Do yourself and others a favor . . . *never* stop growing. And never stop encouraging others to do the same. Life itself is the great schoolmaster. Its curriculum is often very difficult, its lessons painful. Our response is often the key to growth. Every action of ours builds momentum toward growth and development—or toward failure and stagnant immaturity. The growing person responds appropriately to the same pressures faced by everyone else. Unlike many, he has learned to process pressures productively.

Attitude is often the key to this process. The glass is either half full or half empty; it's all a matter of perspective. The bottom-line truth is that our environment itself is largely a reflection of our own attitudes. Growth for most is a decision which begins in the mind. That's where it starts. And that very well may be where you need to start . . . to set a course toward lifelong enrichment. Don't wait until tomorrow!

The Development of Value

Value means nothing and nothing is valuable unless there is an absolute, infinite reference point—a divine north star who is "the way, the truth, and the life." There is such a reference point. There is such a point of ultimate definition. Thank God there is. It was he who said, "Are you not much more valuable than the birds?" God's Word lays it out in black and white. He sent his Son . . . that's why you don't have to worry about tomorrow, what you will eat or drink. His love pursues and provides for what it values.

For many, lovability begins with redefinition. I am not the child of evolution nor the descendant of a primeval beast. As a human being, I bear the image of the eternal God. As a Christian, I have been born into his very family . . . a son or daughter of the King of kings. Napoleon was right: a man does become the man of his uniform. Royal robes do make a difference. Take out your spiritual I.D. card and read again your adoption papers. Note the balance in your spiritual checkbook . . . it's stamped "paid in full."

Building on a healthy, God-given view of my divine pedigree, the next challenge is to develop and exercise practical value. Take inventory of the little things, those special touches that add grace and beauty to life. Resurrect them, give them new life. It is not unusual to discover that we no longer contribute special pluses to the relationship. Gone are the candles, the crystal, the special menus, the favorite dessert, the weekend away, the well cared for home. The secret is to do all that we do "heartily, as unto the Lord." Washing dishes, mowing lawns, changing diapers, and punching a clock take on new meaning if our ultimate motivation is to be found pleasing to him.

Add to those things a renewed concern for beauty . . . beauty of appearance and beauty of the spirit. A literal mirror and a figurative mirror will aid you in this process; the glass and the Good Book will reveal appropriate steps to direct you on your pilgrimage to beauty.

It may be that you're a smashing clothes horse, a genuine jet-setter, handsome, beautiful, but ugly as sin. As someone said, beauty may be skin deep, but ugliness goes all the way to the bone. No amount of costly clothes or cosmetics can hide the ugliness of a caustic, critical, self-righteous spirit. An intimate walk with the Shepherd is the key to releasing his beauty through the full range of our personality. The fruit of his indwelling Spirit is love, joy, peace, longsuffering . . . Most ugliness, most interpersonal strife, can be traced back to the neglect of that all-important relationship with the Lord Christ.

The Day That Changes Your Life

Have you withdrawn into the fetal position and stopped growing? If so, you're probably less lovable. We cannot live on yesterday's manna. Worn out lettermen's jackets and faded press clippings—yesterday's glitter—will not meet the needs of today or tomorrow. Life without growth, without plans, and without purpose is not really life at all.

Perhaps you need to risk, to reach, to act. If you think action is risky, wait until you discover the risk of inaction.

Don't stop growing or encouraging others to grow. You and I value growth, and our hearts follow value. Today's the day to start, and it's always too soon to quit.

Remember, your goal is to stay in the treasure chest of another. To do this, you trust God for the ability to love others in spite of some of their inadequacies, and then make an all-out effort to grow so that others can love you because. Because you are an image bearer of God. Because your practical acts of love are deeply appreciated. Because you add grace and beauty to the lives of your friends and family. Because you are growing and stretching and reaching with each new day that God entrusts into your hands.

What would happen on the day that changes your life? First, *disgust*. This is a good emotion if it drives you in the right direction. Disgust is saying "I've had it with ugliness, with pride, with complacency, with selfishness, and self-centeredness." Disgust focuses on what you don't want.

Second, *decision*. "This is what I intend to do." Decision focuses on what you do want. It involves a God-inspired determination to change direction, to respond appropriately, to take necessary action steps.

Third, *desire*. Like the sign in a thousand locker rooms that reads:

You've Gotta Want It!

TRANSFORMING YOURSELF

You've got to want to change—you must strongly desire to be different. This comes from deep inside.

Fourth, *action*. This is the time for motion! For deeds. To know and not to do is not to know at all. No more fence sitting, no more passing the buck, no more holding back. By God's grace I will reach out and risk. I will plan my work and work my plan.

Fifth, *discipline*. I will resolve to follow through. I will not give up the pursuit of God. Why postpone my better future?

Seek value. Treasure it. You can become more lovable.

4

RESTORING YOUR CONSCIENCE

Big stuff was his name, the barnyard was his domain.

Plumage puffed to the limit, he strutted through life, demanding respect and getting it. A rooster's rooster, he ruled the roost. Even the juvenile roosters, forever challenging and testing, stepped aside when His Majesty strolled by with his high-stepping harem of hens.

He was the biggest and best and he knew it. Didn't the sun itself await his summons each morning? And when he was on the warpath, this cock of the walk terrorized the flock . . . and all nine of us Aldrich kids. That's right, we were afraid of Big Stuff. We'd take him on in a group, but alone? Not a chance! He was a fully equipped African fighting cock, and when Big Stuff crowed, everybody listened.

Early Warning System

Early one morning almost 2,000 years ago, another rooster made history. Two followers of Jesus Christ heard this rooster crow: One listened and lived; one didn't and died. The crowing rooster is an appropriate symbol of an early warning system God has graciously built into each one of us.

It is a system that molds and shapes the inner landscape of our lives.

It is a system with the capacity to open the door to

growing value and lovability—or slam it shut for the rest of our days.

It is a system we call *conscience*. For Peter, Judas, and all mankind, God's love is a rooster that crows.

Like some of the newer cars with their built-in electronic safety systems, conscience is a flashing red light on our spiritual dashboard that tells us something is wrong with the engine. But it's more than a warning. A properly tuned conscience sends out a strong directional signal, guiding the life down productive highways which lead to satisfaction and significance. It is one of God's choice provisions to keep us thinking and acting straight in a crooked, deceitful world. It is a vital part of God's system of quality assurance and quality control.

Properly developed and utilized, the conscience is one of God's gifts to keep the momentum of our lives directed toward success and lovability. In the case of Peter, the crowing rooster routed him back on the course toward pleasing God. As far as Simon Peter was concerned, it got the job done.

Should we then *always* "let our conscience be our guide"?

The answer is no. Our conscience is only as good as the commitments and beliefs which undergird it. It is limited by the truth each individual understands and accepts as a way of life.

A conscience can become callused and indifferent to truth. The apostle Paul describes what happens when men and women willfully shut their ears to the rooster's call:

> having lost all sensitivity, they have given themselves over to sensuality so as to indulge in every kind of impurity, with a continual lust for more.

Conscience is the spiritual equivalent of our physical nervous system. The parallels are most instructive. Our physical system is protective: It registers pain when something goes wrong. If we happen, for instance, to grip a soldering iron by the wrong end, our system telegraphs an urgent ultimatum: Jerk! Flinch! Flee! Get outa there!

It happens every time, unless . . . we happen to have leprosy. The leper has lost feeling. His "rooster," in a sense, is dead. Because there is no warning, this pathetic person suffers injury after injury.

Far worse, however, is the spiritual leper who has lost all sensitivity and willfully hurts himself and others. On the other hand, some actually develop a "hair trigger" conscience which establishes personal boundary conditions that go far beyond the balance and wholesomeness of Scripture. Such folks are bound up in a legalistic life style which leaves them alive—but not really living. They claim truth but produce ugliness. Both of these individuals, the blatant sinner and the self-righteous legalist, need to think through the implications of the rooster's call.

Sometimes, however, we find ourselves wanting to muzzle that rooster that seems to crow at all the inappropriate times—to ignore his warning. Toss that pesky chicken some corn—he'll quit crowing. Eventually he does (at least we don't hear him anymore), and we build momentum toward self-centeredness, turmoil, and failure.

Momentum is an interesting concept involving movement plus acceleration. As momentum builds, movement becomes increasingly difficult to stop or redirect. (Ever try to stop a coasting boxcar?) Translated into life and its choices, momentum looks something like this: Sow a thought (a whole bunch of them), reap an act; sow an act (again, a whole bunch of them), reap a habit; sow a habit, reap a character; sow a character, reap a destiny. Note that our destiny is largely determined by how we think. It takes shape in the mind. Our actions, and ultimately our destinies, are determined by our currently dominant thoughts. Is it any wonder that we are to bring every thought into captivity to Christ (2 Corinthians 10:4-5)? Lovable people are people who think with precision and accuracy about God, themselves, and others.

The conscience, then, is God's provision to direct our thoughts and actions into productive channels. The Spirit of God uses the conscience to convict and confirm, to warn against inappropriate action and confirm appropriate action. It is the walk and wait signals at the intersection. God uses the conscience to keep us in the Cross Walk. The rooster crows when we jaywalk because God cares about our destination.

If the conscience's major function is navigational, then what is the destination? In a word, *Christlikeness*. Boil lovability down to its essence and that's what it is . . . a Christ-like manner of thinking and acting. The deep desire of God's heart is that we would be conformed to the image of his Son. God-flavored people! Lovable people. The Calvary Road leads to the Lord of Calvary. Fortunately, the Bible breaks this glorious destination down into bite-sized chunks.

To learn to love is of utmost importance to those "rich toward God" folks who desire to become more lovable. "The fruit of the Spirit [the ultimate evidence of his presence] is love . . ." "By this shall all men know you are my disciples if you have love for one another . . ." "Be imitators of God, and walk in love . . ."

There's no doubt about it: The Cross Walk is paved with stones of love. The problem? Most of us don't know how to love.

The Priority of Purity

Reflecting on this subject of love, the apostle Paul penned some penetrating thoughts to Timothy, his young friend and associate in the ministry. Timothy was pastoring in a town called Ephesus. The goal of Timothy's ministry, wrote the battle-scarred apostle, was to produce love which springs from *a pure heart, a good conscience, and a life free from hypocrisy* (see 1 Timothy 1:5).

Paul is telling Timothy that when he has preached all his sermons on pneumatology, Christology, hamartiology, soteriology, and eschatology, if his people have not grown in their ability to love and be loved, his ministry has been in vain. Genuine faith expresses its genuineness through visible, tangible acts of love. Decades later the apostle John wrote this same Ephesian church and warned them that unless they recovered their love, God would remove his lampstand from their midst.

First Timothy 1:5 may be the most significant passage ever penned on the subject of love. It penetrates through actions to the heart of the issue. This passage reveals the essential ingredients which must be present *before* we are capable of expressing genuine love. The logical sequence in which these items are presented is crucial to the understanding of Paul's insights.

A pure heart, confirmed by a clear conscience, is the basis for a sincere faith. Love is three dimensional. We are freed to love when we have achieved purity of heart, integrity of conscience, and authenticity of life style. No one has a chance of being a genuinely lovable person without achieving these divinely enabled qualities.

The word translated "sincere faith" comes from the Greek theatre. Actors, in those days, wore masks. This particular term literally means "to speak from under a mask." It came to be applied to people who were hypocrites—inauthentic. An alpha added to the front of the term changed its meaning to " *not* one who speaks from under a mask." In other words, someone who is not a hypocrite, but rather someone who is sincere. Genuinely lovable people aren't hypocrites. They have faced up to the truth about themselves and responded appropriately. That truth may hurt, but even so, maturity is always a return to reality about yourself. The fugitive from truth is also a fugitive from growth and maturity. Paul says that such a fugitive has heart trouble—and his conscience won't let him forget it.

Look at it this way. You can't see my heart. You don't know the condition of my conscience. But you *can* see and judge my life style: It's the visible tip of the iceberg. The rest, as it were, is under water, and only God and I know what lies in those murky depths. His knowledge, furthermore, is complete. Mine is not. While the conscience is *my* monitoring system which apprises me of the condition of my heart, my life style is *your* clue to its condition. If I'm a truly loving person—in word and deed—you can be sure that personal purity lies beneath that loving life style.

Purity is without a doubt the most important ingredient of love. It is love's foundation, its platform, its critical dimension. Lovable people give high priority to purity. Is it any wonder? Love springs from, grows from, flows from purity. As a product of God's indwelling presence, love by its very definition must be pure.

If the paving stones of the Cross Walk are love, the undergirding bedrock is purity.

The Fruits of Impurity

The opposite of purity, of course, is impurity. That which is adulterated, tainted, self-centered, cheapened, and degraded. An impure heart produces a guilt-ridden conscience which encourages a phony life style. In the 1 Timothy passage, Paul is saying that the ultimate aim of ministry is that purity reign in the heart, the control center of our thoughts and actions. Solomon, too, spoke to the heart of this issue:

> Above all else, guard your heart, for it is the wellspring of life (Proverbs 4:23).

It is from the heart, says David's wise son, that the issues and outcomes of life are determined. It determines the direction of our momentum.

The devastation of the impure heart is graphically portrayed by our Lord's teaching in Matthew 15. The newspaper that lands on your porch each morning confirms his words—daily!

> For out of the heart come evil thoughts, murder, adultery, sexual immorality, theft, false testimony, slander. These are what make a man "unclean" (Matthew 15:19-20).

Unappealing as the thought might be, it will be helpful for us to take a closer look at these fruits of impurity, these roadblocks to lovability. And what a bitter basket of fruit it is! A garbage dump of human depravity. So bad, in fact, that nothing short of the new birth can deliver men from their evil effects. Thank God for the crowing rooster to warn us away from these things.

Evil Thoughts

Evil thoughts, the offspring of evil hearts, control both actions and reactions. Mental pictures of physical harm, revenge, and exploitation, if cultivated and watered, will give birth to corresponding actions. Our emotions feed upon our thoughts. "The more I think about it, the more upset I get" illustrates this relationship. Evil thoughts encourage and stimulate evil emotions. It's often a slow, simmering process.

The onset of these dark mental images comes like a slow, silent shadow. It doesn't happen all at once. Think back, if you will, to the days of your courtship. From the first time Mr. or Miss Wonderful registered, you liked what you saw. Caught up in a "cloud built for two," your positive thoughts produced positive emotions ... ecstatic paralysis, to be more exact. You opened car doors for this creature of your dreams. You seated her at the table, wrote her little notes, bought her candy, and brought her flowers. And she loved it. She thought so much about you that she fixed your favorite foods, bought you special gifts, and shared her life with you.

And then you got married. And things changed. New data pushed through the terminal of your mind. Not all of it was positive. Miss Everything wasn't everything after all. Mr. Lovable wasn't always lovable.

And in the midst of your discontent, unhealthy, destructive thoughts—like seeds—found receptivity in the self-centered parts of your heart. Welcomed, warmed, and nurtured, they came to full term and gave birth to selfish, destructive actions.

That's the way of evil thoughts: They eventually give permission for all sorts of self-centered, hurtful attitudes and actions.

Murder

Murder is yet another bitter fruit from the tree of impurity. Murder, of course, means to take life away. This can be done instantaneously, or over a period of years. In the traditional sense, most of us have never murdered anyone. Yet we have taken life away! That cynical, bitter, withdrawn wife was once outgoing, beautiful, and brimming with life. What happened to her? Life was taken away. She was taken for granted; treated as a maid and mistress. And she died inside. Slammed her spirit shut. Men die in similar fashion.

Not to love is to take life away. Self-centered, impure hearts specialize in it. Lovable people add life.

Sexual Immorality

Painted beautiful by contemporary films and novels, sexual immorality is declared ugly and impure by the Lord of the Cross Walk. Modern science has come up with nearly foolproof methods of birth control. The protection offered by these devices, however, does not extend to the conscience. Rooted in impurity, sexual immorality can only produce destruction, pain, and guilt. Guilt is still the burden of an unpaid debt. The rooster's crow haunts many a wandering, homeless, trespassing, dislocated heart. To be used and abandoned is the ultimate depersonalization. Not to treat someone according to his or her true value (as an image bearer of the living God) is to adulterate that person, bringing grief both to the individual and to the heart of the Lord. Impure hearts, however, promote such patterns of living ... and pay the consequences. Lovable people promote sexual purity!

Thievery

Envy and jealousy feed the fires of theft. When individuals afflicted with this type of heart disease attack, watch out for your possessions! Yes, cars, stereos, and silverware disappear. Costly as these losses can be, however, they are nothing compared to the loss of reputation due to thieves who spread gossip and slander.

Working alongside reputation robbers, dream thieves steal hope. Their burglary kits bulge with tools for dismantling dreams, chipping away at hopes, and short-circuiting the deep longings of the heart.

The kid who has been told he's junk, he's worthless, he'll never amount to anything *has been robbed*. Would to God his parents would take his teddy bear, his Legos, or her Raggedy Ann doll instead. But robbed of the stuff of dreams . . . young hearts wither and become old before their time. Many die . . . and are buried years later, victims of an impure heart.

Love is not give and take. It is give and give.

Slander

False testimony and slander also flow from impure hearts. Like delayed-fuse time bombs, these subtle comments and indicting innuendoes blast relationships and crater the basis of intimacy and trust. James doesn't stutter when he talks about the tyranny of the tongue.

> The tongue . . . is a fire, a world of evil among the parts of the body. It corrupts the whole person, sets the whole course of his life on fire, and is itself set on fire by hell (James 3:6).

Fanned into flames by hell, tongues on the rampage set lives on fire. Lovable people "let no corrupt communication proceed out of their mouths, but only such a word as edifies . . ."

Preventive Maintenance

We could linger on among these festering fruits of impurity, but let's open the window and let some positive winds blow though. Purity, lovely and healing in its own right, looks even more beautiful when placed alongside the devastations of a dead conscience and an impure heart.

Lovable folks fight for purity. They pursue integrity and promote holiness. These are the people who appreciate the rooster's call. Aware of the value of conscience, they've developed a preventative maintenance program to guard the function of that vital inner warning system.

In case you didn't know (or hadn't thought about it), preventive maintenance *prevents*. It keeps negative things from happening. Perceiving potential breakdown points and weak spots, it plans and acts to avoid trouble. The motto of the preventative maintenance folks runs like this: "If you're made of dynamite, you don't stoke blast furnaces."

I must know what I'm made of, what I'm allergic to, and then adopt appropriate, responsible patterns of living. Peter said, "Count on me, Lord. Even if everyone else bails out, you can count on Pete." He was dynamite, didn't know it, and a little servant girl lit his fuse. He blew it, and the rooster crowed. The Lord, of course, knew Peter, but Peter thought he "knew better."

Those who move forward in the center of the Cross Walk have developed twenty-four-transistor consciences with many channels. Highly sensitive, they can pick up messages, detect problems, perceive direction, and provide correction. A positive, powerful conscience doesn't come cheap, but is a possibility for all who are serious about pleasing God. Fortunately, the conscience has the capacity to become more powerful as new "transistors" are added.

What kind of conscience-strengthening transistors are we talking about?

The first few are obvious and foundational. A *personal relationship with Christ is the central, indispensable component.* With the new birth, the child of God becomes the temple of the Holy Spirit. He comes to indwell the believer and bring enablement and strength. As we yield to his direction and walk in his paths, we begin the process of becoming new people.

Regular church attendance in a healthy, Bible-teaching church adds a crucial transistor. Significant fellowship with a few caring individuals adds yet another. Fuse in accountability and you add several more. Wire these together with a deep commitment to the Lordship of Christ and the conscience picks up still more power. Commitment and submission to God's Word programs in vital information. Daily devotional study of the Bible and worship of the Lord multiplies the conscience's ability to lock into and hold the divine signal. Regular confession of sin screens out static and conflicting signals. And Scripture memory? Like nothing else, it resets the circuit breakers blown by sin and provides a permanent data base for the directional, decision-influencing functions of the conscience.

"Blessed," said Jesus, "are the pure in heart, for they will see God" (Matthew 5:8). The Greek phrase translated *pure heart* is better rendered as *cleansed heart*. Now, that's good news. When we acknowledge our impurity and seek the forgiveness and cleansing of Christ, we are born into his forever family. We're cleansed, not whitewashed! His indwelling Spirit begins to produce God-flavored fruit in our lives as we respond to his gracious leading. The maturing Christian invites God to perform a white-glove inspection of his heart . . . regularly. Impurity is acknowledged and confessed to the One who is faithful to forgive and cleanse.

One of the most vital elements to traveling the Cross Walk is learning how to respond at that crucial moment when we discern the voice of conscience.

A few pointed questions will help us learn from Peter and the rooster.

CHAPTER
5

RESPONDING TO YOUR CONSCIENCE

We've all seen conscience from the cartoonist's point of view. He's a pesky little guy that rides on your right shoulder whispering admonitions and warnings into your ear. You know, the stern-faced little angel with itty-bitty wings and a halo that always slips down over his eye after scuffling with the miniature devil riding on your *other* shoulder.

We're conditioned by such cute cartoons to think of conscience as a bothersome, minor irritation that we wish would go away—something like an allergy or a game knee.

How often do we think of conscience as a compelling, God-given *force* with the power to affect our destiny? How often are we reminded that conscience—like eyesight and hearing—is a profound gift from a gracious Creator to enable us to live a full and satisfying life?

As we consider how to make the most of this precious capacity, let's begin by asking a simple "why" question. Why does God send crowing roosters into our lives?

Because he loves us.

He cares enough to schedule corrective surgery, knowing full well that sometimes you and I have to hurt before we can heal. God cares cares enough to communicate!

Let that incredible thought sink in. Love is a rooster that crows, that shatters silence, that rejects neutrality, challenges apathy, condemns sin, and affirms righteousness and purity.

Because we don't heed the warnings of Scripture.

"This very night you will all fall away on account of me, *for it is written*: 'I will strike the shepherd, and the sheep of the flock will be scattered'" (Matthew 26:31). That was a warning! And a pretty straightforward one, too. Notice that the living God in human form documents his statement by quoting Old Testament prophetic scriptures.

Thus saith the Lord! How could he make it any plainer? Yet Peter's ears seem sealed by his own self-confidence. "Even if all fall away on account of you, I never will" (Matthew 26:33). Told he would deny his Lord three times, Peter declared, "Even if I have to die with you, I will never disown you" (Matthew 26:35). All the other disciples murmured their assent to these brave words. You can count on us, Lord!

Later, in the Garden, the Lord gave yet another warning. "Watch and pray," he told his little band, "so that you will not fall into temptation. The spirit is willing, but the body is weak."

Again, the message was unmistakable: *Watch*. Stay awake. Stay alert. Be vigilant for the Enemy's attack. Open your eyes. Don't become preoccupied. *Pray*. Lock your gaze on Christ. When all else fails . . . listen . . . lean on your Lord for the strength to resist. Ask him to make both body and spirit willing and strong. Don't try to resist alone!

The message was sent, but the message was not received. They didn't believe the warning; they weren't ready for the attack. Instead, they dropped off to sleep. And when Christ's hour came, "all the disciples deserted him and fled" (Matthew 26:56).

Because we overestimate our own abilities.

Peter's "I never will" says it all. You never will? Watch and pray that you won't. Chances are more than slight that you might. When the fires of temptation or trial are burning hot, resolution and good intentions are prone to go up in smoke. Talk is cheap and overconfidence is dangerous. When opposed by the flesh, determined but ill-advised spirits often sound retreat . . . and the rooster crows.

"If you think you are standing firm," penned Paul, "be

careful that you don't fall!" (1 Corinthians 10:12). That's good biblical counsel, the counsel strong consciences are built upon. Lovable people recognize that their need is not partial, but total and complete. They need, heed, and depend upon God!

Because we are intimidated by peer pressure.

Good intentions fade fast when peer pressure builds. We all feel a need to be accepted. It's tough to stand alone, to be the odd man out, to risk rejection. Picture how Peter felt the pinch. Just as the Lord predicted, his flock fled when the crunch came. Peter followed from a distance, hoping to blend in with the crowd. He didn't. Wouldn't you know it, a little servant girl blew his cover.

> "You also were with Jesus of Galilee!" (Matthew 26:69).

He didn't seem to know what she was talking about. Another gal cornered him by the gate, claiming he was one of Jesus' men. His memory failed him a second time. Punctuating it with an oath, he exclaimed, "I don't know the man!" Later part of the crowd homed in on his Galilean accent and accused him of being a follower of Jesus. Salting his reply with sailor talk, the fisherman once again said, "I *don't know the man!*" This time, the rooster crowed.

Luke tells us that "the Lord turned and looked straight at Peter" (Luke 22:61). What a gaze that must have been. Judging? Compassionate? Questioning? Reaching? Someday we'll know. Certainly Peter never forgot.

Yes, the spirit is willing. But peer-pressured flesh caves in fast. Our good intentions are often neutralized by the conflicting expectations of people. We mean well, but when the instant of crisis crashes in on us, we, like Peter, proclaim "I don't know the man!"

When Does the Rooster Crow?

"Then he began to call down curses on himself and he swore to them, 'I don't know the man!' *Immediately* a rooster crowed" (Matthew 26:74).

Immediately, friend, immediately! Not an hour later,

not a week, not a month. Immediately. God moves quickly to correct his children. He doesn't want us walking any distance down the wrong road. It's in his heart to stop any momentum building toward failure in our lives. He wants to direct us toward becoming more lovable. Aren't you thankful for that!

Will You Always Hear the Rooster?

No.

Words like *neglect, indifference, insensitivity, stagnation, selfishness, rebellion*, and *sterility* help explain why we become spiritually deaf. Hearts harden. Attitudes are layered over by the cement of stubbornness. Signals at the Cross Walk are ignored and then forgotten. Spiritual lepers, we move away from the path which leads to authenticity and lovability. The rooster's voice, however, rings clear to those who are committed to growing in love; who are committed, therefore, to maintaining purity of heart, integrity of conscience, and authenticity of life. These folks welcome the directing, correcting function of the conscience.

How then should we respond when the rooster crows?

Note carefully Peter's pattern, truth which will help us respond appropriately to God's still, small voice.

Peter Principle One:
He Remembered the Word of the Lord.

"Immediately a rooster crowed. Then Peter remembered the word Jesus had spoken . . . " (Matthew 26:74-75). The call of the conscience is first and foremost a call to the truth. Face it we must! *Maturity is always an appropriate response to truth.* The growing, maturing individual welcomes truth—even when it hurts. It often does.

King David writes poignantly about the pain of delaying an appropriate response to known truth. The sad monarch of Israel enrolled in Guilt 101—and paid the full tuition.

> When I kept silent about my sin, my body wasted
>   away
> Through my groaning all day long.
> For day and night Thy hand was heavy upon me;
> My vitality was drained away as with the fever
>   heat of summer.
>   (Psalm 32:3-4 NASB)

Heavy-hearted words! "Thy hand was heavy upon me
. . . my body wasted away . . . my vitality was drained away
. . ." To "remember the Word" and not respond appropriately
is spiritual and emotional suicide. Plunging into preoccu-
pations and mental diversions may mask the issue for a
time, but the emotional energy diverted to the repression
takes its toll. According to David, vitality is replaced by
groaning. Who hasn't groaned? Who hasn't cried out, "if
only, if only." We all feel David's pain. And we've all at-
tempted to run away from it. But we must stop running! At
whatever the cost we must pursue the truth with integrity.
Everyone benefits when we do.

Truth produces beauty, and as the Divine Craftsman,
God intends to make us masterpieces in his eternal gallery.
He knows it is critical that we respond to his beauty-
producing truth. Because he loves us, he will confront us.

Nathan the prophet, acting in God's stead, stuck his
bony finger in David's face and cried out, "You are the man!"
David *was* the man: a liar, an adulterer, a murderer . . . and a
hypocrite. For months he kept silent, held out, didn't con-
fess, and groaned under the weight of his Father's heavy
hand. But God used Nathan to bring David back to truth . . .
and the truth hurt.

Ah, Lord! I know that you use truth to produce beauty, but . . .
wouldn't a thumbnail sketch be adequate for your divine art gallery?
Must I be a masterpiece? Put away the palette knife and use soft char-
coal . . . or crayons.

Aren't you glad he doesn't answer all our prayers?
David discovered that God's Word is living and active,
sharp and penetrating. It cuts through diseased heart tis-
sue like a newly-honed scalpel. It combats corruption and

builds resistance to the inroads of sin. God regularly uses it to get prodigals turned toward home and family. That's one more reason it helps to hide that Word in our hearts.

Peter Principle Two:
He Removed Himself from the Place of Temptation.

". . . and he went outside . . ." (Matthew 26:75).

Peter had denied his Lord in the courtyard—and twice in the gateway. Obviously he wasn't able to handle the pressure. Was the rooster's crow a call to stick around and try to improve his record? Hardly. Peter turned his back on the place where he had stumbled so tragically and hurried out into the predawn darkness.

Joseph is a prime example of one who responded properly to the knock of temptation. He beat a hasty retreat. He knew himself, he knew his limitations, he knew his God. Better to end up in a prison as a righteous man than succumb to an attractive but unrighteous offer. He lost a coat but saved his integrity (Genesis 39). Both David and Peter, however, found themselves at the wrong place at the "right" time . . . and they fell.

Failure promotes failure. If I've already failed . . . why not just one more for the road? If God forgives me once, surely he'll do it again and again and again. And so it goes. Satan, the master of rationalization, encourages this sort of "religious dialogue." He actively promotes discussion of off-limit subjects, of forbidden fruits. Eve bit. The rest is history. *When the rooster crows, an appropriate response includes an inventory of our current environment and associations.* If they're part of the problem rather than part of the solution, it's time to make a rapid exit—even if it means there's no time for explanations.

The rooster's crow is a call to serious and often painful deliberation. With Galilean curse words still echoing between courtyard walls, Peter slipped away into the night. Summoned to do business with God by the call of a humble chicken, he left the scene of the incident. In times of spiritual wreckage it is often quite appropriate and prudent to flee the scene of the incident. Peter "remembered the Word . . . and went outside . . ."

Peter Principle Three: He Repented.

"And he went outside and wept bitterly" (Matthew 26:75).

How the tears must have coursed down those weathered cheeks. Broken-hearted, crushed, ashamed, angry . . . Peter wept—sobbed—as he relived his denial again and again. "I *don't know the man*! Could he have actually said such a thing? And in the hearing of his beloved Lord? What an agony to contemplate! Peter asked himself all the tough questions. He reviewed all the "if onlys." What wouldn't he have given to wake up and discover it was all a bad dream. But it wasn't. If only he could turn the clock back and start over! But he couldn't.

Peter had done the unthinkable, the impossible, the horrible. He'd reached the bottom. He'd sold out his heritage, his values, his reputation . . . and the best Friend a man could ever have. He was a traitor, a hollow braggart, and a coward of the first degree. He'd failed God, his friends, and himself. He wept bitterly.

But it wasn't a bitterness at Jesus, the Romans, the economy, the world situation, or the fisherman's retirement fund. Peter was bitter at himself . . . for not listening, for always pushing, for being so cocky, so sure, so shallow, so unstable, so weak, so rotten, so wretched. His hopes, his dreams, his idealism, his future rode his tears into the dust. It's over, Peter. You're finished. You ended the greatest thing ever to happen on this tired planet earth. Congratulations. Judas committed suicide, why don't you? Certainly the thought must have registered in that dark night of his soul. Have you ever felt like Peter?

Bottled, Peter's tears could not be labeled "Tears of Remorse." Regret? Perhaps, but primarily Peter shed tears of repentance. Could Jesus forgive? Would he cleanse, could he forget, could he welcome Peter again as a friend?

At some point during those sleepless hours of agony,

Peter answered his own question. Hadn't the Lord taught them about forgiven prodigals, adulterers, publicans, and sinners? Come to think of it, Jesus had *always* responded to broken hearts and contrite spirits. What a prayer poor, sad Simon must have uttered that night: holy, salted with tears, wracked with grief, seasoned with joy. Sacred moments. Since the privacy of this scene was protected by God's hovering Spirit, we can only guess at the details of his confession, repentance, and cleansing.

Tears of repentance water the future with hope. They are sweet, life-giving. Tears of remorse, by contrast, are usually hot and bitter with anger and resentment.

A fork in the road confronts the wayward when the rooster crows. He must ultimately choose between the path of repentance and the path of remorse. *Remorseful* people are upset because they got caught and are facing judgment, punishment, or censure. *Repentant* people are grieved because they've failed someone who loves them. The consequences—although not inconsequential—are not the primary concern. Repentant people have called their sin sin. They don't cover it, deny it, minimize it, whitewash it, or blame it on someone else.

The prodigal son got the picture when his bubble burst in the pig pen (Luke 15:11-32). He finally fled the place of temptation. He returned home. He didn't excuse his actions by claiming to have been weaned too early or potty-trained too late. It wasn't grandpa's fault, grandma didn't do it, society didn't let him down, and a low-fiber diet didn't do the damage either.

"Father," he said, "I've sinned against heaven and sinned against you." That's putting the truth on the table. Lovable people learn how to do that. Actually, the prodigal models the only appropriate response to the convicting work of God's Holy Spirit. To confess, literally, means "to say the same thing." God says, "It's wrong." True confession echoes back, "You're right, it *is* wrong." God says, "It's evil." "You're right, it *is* evil!" is the appropriate response. Notice that the prodigal confessed to two people: to his dad and to his heavenly Father, the horizontal and the vertical. What a painful pilgrimage. I see swallowed pride, eaten words, humble pie, fear, and pain all rolled up in one breakthrough experience.

Confession and repentance must not be viewed as some mechanical, mystical formula or the mouthing of religious formulations. Peter's tears put repentance into the high and holy context of the personal and the intimate. When we violate a spiritual boundary condition, it is not the same as violating the impersonal law of gravity. We have grieved a Being whose care for us was clearly demonstrated at Calvary. For us, *Father*, I have sinned . . . says it all. Confession can turn the agony of defeat into the joy of victory.

Peter Principle Four:
He Reaffirmed His Love for the Lord.

Not really knowing what else to do, Peter went back to his fishing boat and nets. He was preoccupied, and the attraction of fishing lay in the fact that he didn't need to think to catch fish. It was second nature. The familiar routine left him plenty of time to ponder, to think, to forget. The wounds of his failure were still fresh . . . but healing.

He wasn't alone. Six fellow disciples joined this memorable fishing trip. Together they fled the terror of the last few hours. I suppose most had already made their private peace with God. This was not a trip intended to replenish the bank account. Disoriented by the sudden turn of events, these men needed to touch base with the familiar, the secure, the timeless . . . the sea, the waves, the creak of the oars, the lonely whine of wind in the rigging. Their conversation is not recorded. I suspect even Peter was at a loss for words. They just needed each other.

Although they kept at it all night, they caught nothing. Not even one little fish for breakfast. A man standing on shore shouted out to the boat and suggested they try the water on the right side of the vessel. Under normal circumstances . . . a rather stupid suggestion. Well, why not? Couldn't lose anything. Peter and his men plunged the nets over the starboard side—and immediately one hundred and fifty-three large, divinely guided fish crammed into the net. Even the seasoned fishermen were taken aback by their size and number. Peter shouted, "It's the Lord" and dove overboard. Unable to lift the hefty catch over the gunwales, the rest of the men towed the bulging net to the beach.

A memorable meal climaxed this, our Lord's third postresurrection appearance to his disciples. Three times he had appeared, three times he confirmed his loyalty to them, three times he had proven his faithfulness. Following their simple breakfast, Jesus turned to Peter and asked a probing question . . . three times.

"Peter, do you love me?"

He had denied his Lord three times. Now he was being asked three times to affirm his love.

"Do you love me?"

Is there any other question? Is this not life's most important question? To each question Peter humbly replied, "Lord, you know that I love you." Gone was the boastful arrogance of the garden. The sword-swinging warrior's ears were finally open. He listened intently.

His heartfelt reply was deliberate and authentic. He did love his Lord.

Mark it well, the crowing of the rooster marks the coming of the Son! He comes to you and me with the same question. He raises the same issue. He seeks the same assurance.

You failed me, you denied me. If you love me, you'll keep my commandments. Your violation of that trust brings your love into question.

The Lord turned to Peter's boat and the pile of prize fish and said, "Peter, do you love me more than these? Am I really first in your priorities . . . the object of your affections? Will you sacrifice these for me?" Do we love him more than our careers, our securities, our worldly treasures?

Boil it down and the issue is always love. We can't serve two masters. Never could, never will.

God wants us to say it: "Yes, Lord, I do love you more than these. I do love you . . . in spite of all my denials, my inconsistencies, my disappointing failures. I do love you, I want to please you, and I want you to be proud of me. I long above all else someday to hear you say, 'Well done, my good and faithful servant.'"

When the rooster crows, be prepared for the coming of the Son.

Peter Principle Five:
He Was Recommissioned for Service.

"Again Jesus said, 'Simon son of John, do you truly love me?' He answered, 'Yes, Lord, you know that I love you.' Jesus said, 'Take care of my sheep'" (John 21:16).

Peter's reaffirmation of love was the basis of his recommission. Oh, the joy of restoration to fellowship and service!

Centuries before this seaside encounter, the Word of the Lord came to Jonah *a second time*, "Arise and go to Nineveh." He'd run, he'd hidden, he'd failed, he'd denied. But God gave his reluctant spokesman a second chance. He's the same today as he was then . . . a God of second chances. His call upon you is irrevocable.

After his recommissioning, Simon, the unstable one, the impetuous one, the vacillating one, became *petros*. Peter. The rock.

Never Too Soon to Listen

Two people heard that rooster of old. One resisted and died; the other repented and lived. Although Judas' suicide was relatively quick, in reality he died by inches. Each time he heard the Master speak and was unresponsive, each time he experienced Christ's love and was unmoved, each time he witnessed the Lord's power and was indifferent— he died a bit. He built momentum toward failure and became one of the most unloved people in human history. Slowly but surely the death shroud lowered itself upon him until it was too late. He sowed an act and reaped a destiny.

Satan counteracts the voice of conscience by whispering, "It's too soon." Too soon to set things right; too soon to slow life's pace long enough to get serious about God; too soon to climb off the merry-go-round and dilute your fun. Listening to this deceptive voice, many wait, and the wreckage builds until Satan whispers, "Sorry, it's too late. You've blown it, God won't forgive. You're beyond hope. It's impossible for you to love and to become lovable." Remember, Satan is a liar.

Thank God for roosters! Immediately a rooster crowed and Peter remembered the Word. People who develop the habit of responding to God's words become Christ-flavored people. Lovable people. People who are truly alive, authentic, beautiful, and sincere.

So seek to heed his words; seek to stand strong and whole-hearted for his name. He's made every provision for your success.

But when you fall, when you hear the rooster, come running back into the arms of your Lord.

He'll be right where you left him.

PART TWO

TRANSFORMING YOUR WORLD: THE REST OF THE STORY

CHAPTER

6

LOVE ENCOURAGES GROWTH

"**D**o I love you because you are beautiful . . . or are you beautiful because I love you?"

A most interesting question. In fact, a rather profound one. Let's play with it a bit. How about this: "Do I love you because your are *lovable*, or are you lovable because I love you?" There certainly are folks whom I love because they are lovable. They make it easy to love them. In fact, it's a snap. I hope there are some people who love me because they perceive me to be lovable. They love me because of what I am. I'm certain there are some who love me in spite of what I am. I'd like to believe that the "in spite of" crowd is diminishing—that they're being converted to "because of" folks.

"Are you beautiful/lovable because I love you . . . ?" In other words, does my love contribute to your beauty? Can my care and compassion alter your character? If I love, can you become more lovable? What role does love play in the growth of another individual?

If marriage is like a garden in which one person plants the seed of his life in the soil of another's life, what happens if that soil is full of weeds, thorns, and thistles? Personality is a product of relationships. We become like the people we associate with. The gorgeous bride often becomes the bitter wife . . . because of the weeds. The soil in which we are nurtured is an important factor in our growth—or lack of it. In Ephesians 3:17, Paul underscores this fact when he reminds us that God has planted us in the soil of his perfect love. To whom are you a soil?

Perhaps you heard of the Hittite who graduated from Hittite A & M and decided to follow the tradition of his distinguished alma mater and become a farmer. He bought some land in Texas and went to work. He plowed and cultivated it, getting it ready to plant. In the course of time he decided to raise chickens. Planted 'em head first in rows. Wasn't long until he experienced crop failure. But these A & M boys weren't ones to give up easily. He planted a second crop ... this time feet first. The planted chickens stirred up dust a little longer, but eventually kicked the bucket.

Now this young farmer was really perplexed. Suddenly a light bulb went off. As a graduate of this prestigious university, he could write the extension bureau, explain his experiment, and receive counsel from the experts. And so he did. He grabbed a felt tip pen and a pad of paper. Sitting at his chrome-legged, formica-topped kitchen table, he put it all on paper. The envelope addressed and sealed, he walked the gravel driveway to the mailbox, tossed it in, put up the red flag, and waited. Each day he walked that long driveway to the box in anticipation of his answer. Finally the long-expected letter arrived. In the upper left-hand corner was the return address: Hittite A & M, Extension Bureau. He knew he had his answer.

Rushing back to the old farm house, he ran to the kitchen, grabbed a knife, and slashed open the envelope. The letter was short and to the point. It said, "Please send soil sample."

If the corn crop's dying it's not a bad idea to check the soil. In the case of chickens, check something else. Have you ever thought of love as soil? It's a most instructive illustration of what is necessary to grow a life. How fertile is the soil of your life? What are the ingredients of healthy, growth-producing soil? What are the critical elements which stimulate the growth of another individual? Who are those people whose roots are drawing from the soil of your life? Are they healthy? Malnourished? What steps can you take to head off crop failure in the lives of those close to and dependent upon you? Tough questions! The Bible has the answers. Tucked away in Paul's note to his pastor-friend Timothy we find this clue:

"speaking the *truth* in *love*, we will in all things *grow* up into him [Christ] . . ." (Ephesians 4:15).

Three key elements come together: truth, love, and growth. The whole context is talking about no longer being infants, but growing up as each part of the Christian community contributes its part. Truth and love are the essential ingredients, growth the desired outcome. As we will discover, Paul's big idea is that *when truth is communicated through a love-flavored person, growth is the expected result.* Let's look first at this concept of growth.

Growth: The Intent of the Growth-Stimulating Person.

The phrase "in all things" indicates Paul is interested in much more than Bible knowledge or spiritual insights. He has in mind the total growth of the total person: spiritually, emotionally, mentally, socially, and physically. Growth is not only an outcome of the proper blending of love and truth, it is also the concern of those committed to discipling others.

How can I really love another if I am unconcerned about that individual's growth? It is the intent of every true lover to use every resource at his or her command to stimulate growth.

Guido Reni was a famous portrait artist who was noted for his paintings of beautiful women. One day an Italian aristocrat came into his studio and was quite taken by the portraits. Enraptured, he turned to Guido and said, "I'd surely like to meet your model!" With that Guido summoned a rather coarse-looking individual from the back of the studio and invited him to be seated before a blank canvas. Guido started to paint the head of a beautiful woman. The Italian aristocrat was incredulous. "You don't mean to say," he exclaimed, "that this homely person is your model?"

Guido continued painting. The face on the canvas grew in its beauty. Finally, the master spoke.

"You see, your excellency, it makes no difference who the model is if the artist has honorable intentions."

Growth is an honorable intention. How can I resist someone who comes across as genuinely interested in my personal growth and development? Such interest produces lots of tug! It shows you care.

As we observed in a previous chapter, to be "rich toward God" is to exchange my life for what he has declared to be important: his word and people. When the success of another is at least as important as my own personal achievement, my intentions are becoming honorable.

What is your intent, your purpose? It determines everything! If it's noble, you'll become noble in its accomplishment. How will your responses to that husband, wife, child, or friend be different if their growth is your number one concern? Before you make the comment, before you act or react, ask yourself the question: "Will what I am about to say or do contribute to this person's growth?" If it won't, don't say it or do it! Lovable people run regular "growth checks" before they react or respond.

A growth focus presupposes a commitment to ongoing personal development. It is not enough to be concerned about someone else's growth. As we have seen in a previous chapter, lovable people continue to grow in practical value. They cultivate the aesthetics of body and soul. As they grow, they increase their ability to contribute to the growth of others. Our Lord put it well when he reminded us that "when the pupil is fully taught, he will be *like* his teacher." Like him. Growth produces growth. If we're committed to growth, if that is our *intent*, then truth and love will be given top priority.

Truth: The Content Used by the Growth-Stimulating Person.

Why would we be committed to anything less than truth? It is only truth that can set us free. Obviously, then, mature people are truth hunters. Truth is the basic stuff of growth. Jesus said, "I am . . . the truth." He is the infinite reference point of the universe, the starting point for the only valid world view, the only perfect master/teacher. His word is either the final authority . . . or he's the greatest fraud who ever lived. After all, he claimed to be God, to be sinless, to exist before Abraham, to be the only way to his Father.

"Speaking the truth . . ." is the critical factor in growth. Since only seven percent of effective communication is verbal, certainly *living* the truth is even more significant. John made it clear in his epistle that a lover seeks to align lives with truth. Lovable people are always seeking to promote obedience to what Holy Scriptures teach and proclaim.

Our culture floods us with lies. The very word *advertisement* means to "advert," to lure away our attention by means of attractive—and often deceptive—claims. It isn't true that if you use a certain brand of toothpaste you will be cruising the Caribbean in a beautiful yacht. It isn't true that you can sleep around with multiple partners and enjoy a "good" life. It isn't true that you can walk around sipping a cool drink from morning to night and stay sober, build healthy relationships, and find satisfaction in life. It isn't true that buying a new car or a new home will ease eternal heartaches. It isn't true that you can relegate your faith to the corners of your life and be a satisfied, fulfilled, productive person.

Man's ultimate aim is to glorify God . . . period. There is no plan B. There is no viable alternative to exchanging my life for what God has declared to be important. To choose to be rich toward myself rather than God is the ultimate folly. I glorify God by obeying him, by doing that which is pleasing to him, by skillfully handling the truth. As Moses taught, the truth must be upon my heart before I introduce it into the home. Love begins its operation from a heart that is pure.

Are you open to the truth . . . about yourself? The truly lovable person refuses to run from the facts. Rather, he welcomes them, painful as they may be at times. Maybe others aren't excited about truth because we aren't. Perhaps they're indifferent because we are. Could it be they haven't grown because we haven't? Perhaps all they do is watch TV . . . because that's all we do. Maybe they're critical and hard to live with because . . . oh, my. Now that's getting close to home.

As an agent of truth we are to intersect the lives of others in such a way that truth impacts and changes their lives. But that does not mean we are given a blank check to communicate that truth in any old way we please. Far from it! Paul's passage teaches that truth is to be communicated "in love." Truth without love is brutality. Effective communication is the blending of proper content (truth) with the proper context (love).

Love: The Context Established by the Growth-Stimulating Person.

Love is the soil, the context in which the truth comes alive. If you visualize truth as a seed, love is the soil in which the seed flourishes and produces growth. No soil, no growth? I think that's true. There are some important principles which grow out of the delicate balance between love and truth.

First, there is a correlation between truth and growth. There's no growth without truth. Lovable people make understanding and living of truth a top, number one priority.

Second, long before I communicate content (truth) I must build context (love). Nothing has meaning without context. In a very real sense I forfeit the right to lay down the law if I haven't "built up the soil." This is especially true if my intent is growth, not winning or proving my point. You've probably already learned that there is no such thing as an individual victory in a marriage relationship. If you win, you lose.

The thing that makes discipline effective is not a quick hand with the paddle. Discipline becomes effective when the child is moved by the fact that he's disappointed someone who loves him. Discipline outside the context of love usually produces bitterness and resentment.

Scripture does not tell us to "truth" our neighbors; it tells us to love them. We're not told to "evangelize" them, we're told to love them. We are told to build the context and then be ready "to give an answer to every man that asks you the reason for the hope that is in you."

Third, the impact of truth is in direct proportion to the experience of love. In other words, truth builds up tug when it's surrounded by love. Love is the frosting on the cake, the ice cream on the pie. That's why it's so important to focus on building and stockpiling context. Truth is easier to receive when it's surrounded by love. And that leads us to the next principle.

Fourth, there is a direct relationship between the acceptance of truth and the assurance of love. If I come to you with something that is absolutely true, but I come with a chip on my shoulder, chances aren't too good you will accept and respond appropriately to the truth. There probably isn't much difference between the nutritional value of barracks food and what fine restaurants serve. It's all in the presentation, the context, if you please. More often than not, it is not *what* is said that creates the problem, but *how* it is said.

If I sense that you really care, that you are committed to my growth and development, I will not only hear the truth, I will also very likely respond to it, learn from it. Remember, our goal is not simply to establish a truth delivery system. Our task is not finished when truth is delivered. We really haven't accomplished much if the truth is just heard. In fact, if truth isn't acted upon we have a tendency to become immune to it. Because Capernaum heard but didn't act upon the truth, the Lord told them their judgment would be worse than that coming upon the inhabitants of Sodom and Gomorrah—who never heard.

Fifth, the loving person is greatly concerned with both the external and internal circumstances surrounding the communication of truth. The lovable person does an internal audit before he says anything. Three questions come to mind:

Do I really care?

Is it true?

Will it help?

He checks the context for love, the content for truth, and his basic intention. He proceeds if he can answer yes to each of the questions.

The circumstances surrounding the communication of truth should be carefully monitored. Love should be the guiding principle. Before actual communication takes place, there are some tests which should be administered.

The "Why" Test

Why we say something needs to be checked out before we utter a word. The loving person checks out his motives. He asks, "Why do I feel it is necessary to drop this information, to communicate this truth?" Is it to win, to dominate, to impress, to overrule? Could it be jealousy, envy, or hate which motivates me to "share the truth"? Am I just name-dropping to impress? Is it a genuine prayer concern, or am I just using the smoke screen of prayer to pass on gossip? If you can't improve on silence . . . don't try.

The "How" Test

How you communicate directly influences the reception of what you have to say. So much is tied up in tone of voice. I'll catch one of my kids being a bit impudent with mom and suggest they not talk to her that way. Their reply? "All I said was . . . " True, they repeat the verbal message without error . . . but they change their tone of voice. The sassy overtones have suddenly disappeared. It's not the same message.

Everyone has the right to be treated with dignity: mom, dad, and yes, the little ones, too. Why scold, why harangue, why wave your finger in their faces? Turn off your scold, eliminate the anger, put yourself in their shoes. If an adult came to you and communicated to you like many folks do to their kids, how would you respond? Do you think the kids like it? An adult can leave the room, shut the door, or fight back. A kid has no recourse. If he responds like an adult, he gets cratered!

I listened to Ruthe, my wife, instruct our still-sleeping son about making his bed. Mind you, he's still in it and hasn't even started his motor for the day. The words were fine. It was the scolding tone of voice that caught my attention. Message delivered, I asked her how she expected Stephen to respond. Did she expect him to jump out of bed fairly frothing at the mouth and with ecstasy proclaim, "Right on. Thanks for reminding me. I can hardly wait to make my bed!" Hardly. The response is greatly influenced and shaped by the how of the message. Lovers take the how seriously.

The "Where" Test

In front of others usually isn't the right "where." Truth is often rejected because we are not sensitive to place and attendant circumstances. Nobody wants to be told he failed the exam with twenty others listening in to the delivery of the "truth." Discretion is the key.

It's likely that the wife doesn't want her upcoming surgery brought up for conversation in a group of people. It is probably not best to severely rebuke a child in front of others, especially his peers. If you choose to, you have pretty well predetermined his response. Don't expect a positive response from a negative setting.

In evangelism, if you choose to buttonhole someone who is in a crowd of his buddies and deliver the truth, chances are very good he'll reject the truth, even though he may be personally interested in what you have to say.

At breakfast on an isolated beach was the appropriate time and place to confront Peter with his denial of the Lord. Deep down he wanted to be confronted with the truth. He knew he had failed, and he wanted to talk it out . . . but not in front of the whole world.

Sharing a piece of your mind with your mate in front of the kids is usually not an appropriate place or time. The fact the problem has been aired in front of the children may preclude a positive response. If our goal is to deal with truth in such a way that it contributes to mutual growth, we must take the where seriously. Sometimes "later, dear" is the best and most productive response.

The "When" Test

We often reduce the impact of truth because we are insensitive to timing. Timing can be wrong if we're surrounded by people. Timing can also be wrong if our mood, our frame of mind is not receptive to truth. Let tempers cool, let perspective return before the full weight of the truth is delivered. After the storm is usually the best "when" for both parties. Both the offended and the offender can cool down. Lovable people give others the opportunity to get it together before they face them with the truth.

Lovers are sensitive to the communication context. Try it on for size. How would those significant others in your life respond if you worked harder on building context, providing assurances of love and care, and backed off from confronting them with so much "truth"? Does it make any difference how truth is served? When and where it is served? Why it is served? How sensitive are you to some of these contextual factors? Does your tone of voice really contradict the intent of your heart? Would growth and development come more quickly if you focused on some of the positive truths about the person and backed off from highlighting the negatives?

Would growth accelerate if you spent more time driving out fear, building confidence, and encouraging positive relationships? The seed is truth, the soil is love, the proper relationship between them produces growth. If the soil isn't right, truth isn't going to produce much fruit.

Love Is the Filter

Love is the filter for all truth. Before truth is communicated it needs to pass the already discussed internal and external audit. The why, when, where, and how tests are like gags or muzzles. If the desire to say something can't pass the why test, nothing should be said—the motive for communicating the truth was probably not an honorable intention. Likewise, if the desire to communicate something can't pass the when, where, and how test, the truth should not be delivered! "Let no unwholesome communication proceed out of your mouth," Paul cautions us, "but only such a word as is good for edification, according to the need of the moment." Good advice! Love communicates only that which builds.

7

LOVE FORTIFIES TRUTH

Truth is to be love-flavored. We've established that much.

But what, then, does love "taste" like? How can you and I evaluate whether our words are loving or not? Is there a standard by which we can measure ourselves—a landmark on the horizon that can give us our bearings?

As a matter of fact . . .

The thirteenth chapter of Paul's first letter to the Corinthians rolls back the ground fog, clears away the horizon-obscuring brush, and presents a wondrous vista . . . soaring peaks and surging rivers . . . the compelling landscape of true, biblical love.

If we are to "speak the truth in love," then our speaking must be controlled and influenced by the facets of love described in this great love chapter. Each quality of love is a vital ingredient of the kind of soil which stimulates healthy growth. We speak, therefore,

> with patience because "love is patient"
> with kindness because "love is kind"
> without envy because "love does not envy"
> without boasting because "love does not boast"
> without pride because "love is not proud"
> without rudeness because "love is not rude"
> without self-seeking because "love is not self-
> seeking"

without anger because "love is not easily
    angered"

without being "historical" because "love keeps
    no record of wrongs"

without delighting in evil because "love rejoices
    in the truth"

with protection because "love always protects"

with trust because "love always trusts"

with hope because "love always hopes"

with perseverance because "love always
    perseveres."

Stated negatively, we have nothing to say if:

we are impatient
we are unkind
we are boastful
we are prideful
we are rude
we are self-seeking
we are angry
we are "record keepers"
we delight in evil
we have no commitment to protect
we do not trust
we do not communicate hope
we have no commitment to persevere.

Each quality contributes to the fertility and growth-producing ability of the soil. Each one, if present, adds impact and vitality to the truth. Each quality strongly influences the reception of truth. If love is absent, truth is less likely to result in growth. Each quality is like a filter. Filters screen out or stop that which is undesirable or destructive. The loving communicator uses Paul's list for quality assurance and quality control. Any attempt to speak the truth which would violate the spirit of love described by Paul is counterproductive. Wouldn't it be wonderful if before we ever spoke we asked ourselves, "Am I patient, am I kind, am I envious, boastful, proud . . . ?" We must develop and use this mental checklist if our intent is growth and speaking the truth in love.

Love Is Patient

Patience is a key ingredient in the soil of love. If we are speaking the truth in an impatient manner, we should not anticipate it to produce growth. If patience is missing, growth is hindered. Lovable, growth-oriented people have learned the secret of patience. Surround the truth with patience, and it will bear fruit.

We all know this is true. A preoccupied, impatient person trying to communicate turns all of us off. The presence of impatience is a red flag to the sensitive communicator.

I'm about to communicate something. I'm impatient. Is the "when" now? No. If I am to speak the truth in a context of love, I must wait until I'm under control, until I have an attitude of patience. Speaking the truth with patience, I can anticipate growth. Patience multiplies the impact of truth. Impatience hinders the process. Imagine how much truth would not be communicated if we took the patience filter seriously! It would muzzle many unfortunate conversations.

> How poor are they that have not patience?
> What wound did ever heal, but by degrees?
> —William Shakespeare

> They also serve who only stand and wait.
> —John Milton

Love Is Kind

Truth must be sugarcoated with kindness! Kindness stimulates growth. It's one of the most vital ingredients of the soil of love. Unkindness kills growth. If we really care about growth, delivering truth in an unkind manner is an exercise in futility. If we just want to win—or prove our point—I guess it doesn't really matter. An old Chinese proverb says, "Better do a kindness near home than go far to burn incense." Kindness is a powerful force for changing behavior. How can you resist someone who presents you with the truth in a patient, kind manner?

You have something to say. Something needs to be said. You're in an ugly, very unkind mood. Can you speak the truth in love? Of course not. The kindness filter eliminates your right to say anything! If it's unkind, it isn't love. Think how much talking would be ruled out if we used this filter—and didn't say anything unless kindness ruled our hearts. Lovable folks seem to abound in kindness. We shouldn't be surprised!

> Kind hearts are the garden,
> Kind thoughts are the roots,
> Kind words are the blossoms,
> Kind deeds are the fruits.
> —John Ruskin

Love Does Not Envy

The Greek root for envy means "to seethe or boil." Anyone not guilty? Love will not tolerate it! Try speaking the truth through the envy filter and see what happens. You might be surprised by what you don't say. Envy-tainted truth will not—cannot—produce growth. If you love God and love people, you will choke off envious words before they fall from your lips. Envy is simply abhorrent to a lovable person.

The neighbor with the new car, the lady with the new dress, the country club membership, and the yacht are all potential victims of our envy. It's so easy to speak the truth and throw daggers at the same time. But it's destructive, and it's sinful. Love and envy are mutually exclusive. Let's keep them this way!

> Envy is a coal come hissing hot from hell.
> —Philip J. Bailey

> Envy, the meanest of vices, creeps on the ground like a serpent.
> —Ovid

Envy is uneasiness of the mind, caused by the consideration of a good we desire, obtained by one we think should not have it before us.
—John Locke

Love Does Not Boast

The bedfellows of *boast* make it clear why it is opposed to love. Listen to some of its cousins: vaunt, bluff, swagger, brag, chauvinism, pretension, hot air, and exaggeration.

We don't like people who wear these words! We don't put them on our top ten list. It takes large doses of *agape* just to tolerate such actions. It's okay for turkeys to preen, strut, flourish, and generally show off. People who do it, however, are real turkeys.

To boast is to flaunt the superiority of some possession, position, or product. It is an attempt to demean the other by highlighting an area of personal strength. Boasting is often a positioning maneuver. Whatever else one might like to say, when it's mixed with truth, it doesn't deliver. Are you apt to accept and integrate truth delivered by a boastful, arrogant communicator? I have my doubts!

Love Is Not Proud

Pride is another weed, a truth-killer of the greatest magnitude. Its companions are an ugly brood. They include haughtiness, pomposity, and conceit. Certainly there is a legitimate pride. We understand that. Paul is referring to an inordinate, self-seeking, self-elevating self-inflation.

Such pride dulls the impact of truth. To present the truth in love is to present it with gentleness and humility. Humility opens the spirit of others to the truth. Humility builds receptivity, pride destroys it.

Again, what is our intent? Do we want to encourage growth? Growth is the product of truth being integrated into one's life and experience. How do we get truth into life? By assuming a posture of humility, and from that mindset living and teaching truth.

Love is neither anxious to impress nor does it cherish inflated ideas of its own importance.
—J. B. Phillips

There is perhaps no one of our natural passions so hard to subdue as *pride*. Disguise it, struggle with it, beat it down, stifle it, mortify it as much as one pleases, it is still alive, and will every now and then peep out and show itself.
—Benjamin Franklin

The fruit of the Spirit is . . . meekness.
—the apostle Paul

Love Is Not Rude

The Septuagint (Greek translation of the Old Testament) uses the term *rude* of a person who is without clothes, naked and bare. It comes from a root which means "shameful, unpresentable, indecent, rude."

Now we've left preaching and gone to meddling. The hamburger has hit the fan! Men and women who are coarse, tactless, vulgar, uncultivated, and loud have lost their tug. They're not particularly lovable, either. Rude people have neglected the aesthetics of the spirit. Value-seeking hearts usually detour around rudeness.

Rudeness is one of the most powerful enemies of growth. Are you inclined to pay much attention to the preaching of rude people? Not me. I usually tune them out. To be rude is certainly not to treat someone according to his true value. On the contrary, to be rude is to treat someone like junk. Nobody needs that. Life is tough enough as it is without being subject to someone's rudeness. A*gape* empowered people attempt to love in spite of the rudeness, but it's a sizable challenge! It takes a high level of maturity to put up with it.

Rude people, of course, need our love and concern. Sometimes our love will be expressed by letting them know, in a spirit of humility, how they are coming across. Love may overlook inadequacies, but it never ceases to desire the removal of those inadequacies. Sometimes God fingers us and says, "thou art the man, you tell him he's rude." If I assume, by God's grace, the qualities of 1 Corinthians 13 and communicate truth, the ball's in his court. I am not responsible if the truth about his rudeness offends him. I am responsible for the manner, the way in which I communicate it. I must accept the blame if it was shared at the wrong time or place or in an inappropriate manner.

Replay some of your recent tapes . . . your conversations with that wife, husband, child, or peer. How effectively was truth communicated? You got the message across. You swear that you told the truth, the whole truth, and nothing but the truth, so help you God. Good. You can put your hand down. But now let's do a "manner" check. Were you patient, kind, free from envy, boasting, pride, and rudeness? You'll have to think about that?

Please do.

> Love has good manners.
> —J. B. Phillips

Love Is Not Self-Seeking

Selfishness or self-centeredness confronts us with the "big why" question. Like few of the other facets of love, this one hits at motive. It asks, "why do you feel compelled to 'speak the truth?' "

Paul says that real love isn't selfish. Instead, love acts to shut down selfishness. Let's face it, truth wrapped in selfishness is pretty hard to swallow.

Selfishness is a way of life which leads to death. Our barn-building farmer was selfish. God called him a fool and put his life on fast forward. But it doesn't always happen that way. Sometimes death comes much slower. Selfishness is a poison which kills creativity, beauty, spontaneity, and growth.

The New Birth allows us to put off the wardrobe of death . . . selfishness being part of it . . . and put on the wardrobe of grace. The essence of life is to give it away. If we hoard it, we'll lose it; if we give it away, we'll save it. In Romans 12 Paul challenges each Christian to present himself as a "living sacrifice" to God. When we do . . . and we must . . . we begin to build momentum toward becoming a lovable, much-loved person. Nothing wrong with that!

The opposite of selfishness is service. Servants are irresistible. They're powerful people. Paul could say, "Though I am free and belong to no man, I make myself a slave to everyone, to win as many as possible" (1 Corinthians 9:19). What is he saying? No service, no souls! You see, we are the message. God's communication strategy has always been to clothe an idea in a person—an individual who tastes like the qualities of love described for us in 1 Corinthians 13. If that's our flavor, we can expect to see truth take root all around us. Selah!

Love does not insist on its own way (RSV).

Love does not pursue selfish advantage (Phillips).

Love is never selfish (NEB).

Love Is Not Easily Angered

Anger is only one letter short of danger. When we lose control, we generally lose. It's tough to attempt to communicate truth when we've blown our circuit breakers. It's not that the Bible forbids anger—there are times when it's the appropriate response. What Paul probably had in mind here was a "short fuse," although the word *easily* is not in the Greek text.

Love isn't touchy, irritable, easily provoked. How much communication would be eliminated if we shut down before we blew up? The lovable person has learned how to count to ten. He attempts to be under control before he delivers the truth. If growth is the intent, anger must be brought under the Spirit's control.

Love is not touchy (Phillips).

Love is not quick to take offense (NEB).

Love Keeps No Record of Wrongs

What an incredible insight. If we love someone we must forfeit the right to be "historical." No one has the right to go on archaeological expeditions into the past and dredge up garbage.

"You mean I've got to empty the skeleton closet?"

Clean it out!

"You mean I can't remind them . . . I can't dangle it in front of them?"

That's what I mean!

"Can't be historical?"

No chance!

People who would make others prisoners of the past shatter more relationships and generate more bitterness and sorrow than you can imagine. When you speak the truth in love, the sins of the past aren't part of the conversation. Busting people over the head with yesterday's mistakes does not stimulate growth. Nor does it evidence much of what the Bible would call care.

I once had a lady come in for counseling who had a list which extended back *fifteen years*. It had the past wrongs of her husband listed by date, time, and the nature of the offense. I kid you not. It was at least an inch thick. When I showed her that "love keeps no record of past wrongs," she got up and walked out. I didn't like her anyway. It's hard to like people who hold grudges, who won't forgive and forget. They've lost their tug.

Love does not keep account of evil (Phillips).

Love keeps no score of wrongs (NEB).

Love Does Not Delight in Evil but Rejoices in the Truth

The truth may be that someone has been evil . . . very evil. We may be impelled to share the truth of that evil. If in sharing it our intention is the growth and development of the one hearing it, we cannot rejoice or gloat or make light of the wickedness. Generally, we gloat because we enjoy judging the other fellow or because his failure makes us appear superior. Either response is wrong and is out of character with what love would do.

The lovable person rejoices in what is right and true. He knows what to get excited about. He is overjoyed when truth prevails, when right is done.

How do you react to the sight or sound of evil? What about those "prayer requests" that get passed along over the phone—the ones where all the juicy details are included in the package. The ones passed on in living color. Is that not rejoicing in evil? When we rejoice, we are announcing to the world what it is that brings us delight. Rejoicing is the outward evidence of what turns us on. If we rejoice in evil it's because we delight in it.

If our motivation for communicating truth is that we delight in evil, then our communication will not benefit those who hear it.

> Love does not rejoice at wrong, but rejoices in the right (RSV).

> Love does not gloat over other men's sins, but delights in the truth (NEB).

> Love does not gloat over the wickedness of other men. On the contrary, it is glad with all good men when truth prevails (Phillips).

Love Always Protects

Love throws a blanket of silence over others' faults. It shares truth with an attitude of protection and permanency. It is unshockable and enduring in its support.

Sometimes we have to deliver some heavy truth. If we come with an attitude of support, the truth has a much greater chance of penetrating and bringing about change.

Lovable people let others know that they are on their team, that they will root for them . . . no matter what. I put it in writing for my youngsters. Each month my children get a note from dad which goes into a special notebook. They know that their parents will stand behind them.

Love bears all things (RSV).

Love knows no limits to its endurance (Phillips).

There is nothing love cannot face (NEB).

Love Always Trusts

Most interpret this to mean that love is not suspicious of fellow man and refuses to yield to the suspicions of doubt. The lovable person prefers to be too generous in his conclusions, crediting his neighbor with good intentions he might not even possess. And if we err, isn't it better to err on the side of grace?

The true lover is ready and willing to believe the best. He has a trustful disposition, ascribing the best of motives to others in their actions.

Do you impute motives and desires to others which are not true, which are unfair and destructive? How does a suspicious, distrustful attitude influence the communication of truth? When you are discussing the rightness or wrongness of a particular incident or issue, don't you prefer to be taken at face value, to be given the benefit of the doubt? Are you apt to respond to the truth if your integrity is always under scrutiny?

How desperately we need someone to believe in us . . . even during those times when there doesn't seem to be much to believe in. We welcome truth when it comes from those who trust us.

Love believes all things (RSV).

Love knows no end to its trust (Phillips).

There is no limit to its faith (NEB).

Love Always Hopes

In the blackest of hours, when the heavy door of finality seems determined to swing shut—love gets a foot in the door. Love lets hope shine as a bright sliver—however thin—into the gloom of a darkened room.

Love has the ability to expect good things from its

fellow man even though the evidence may seem to the contrary.

Lovers are hope injectors. They restore souls. Lovable people refuse to let you quit, won't let you give up. Speaking the truth in love means that no matter how difficult the issue, love continues to project hope. Communication should never be devoid of hope. Truth wrapped in hope has a good chance of accomplishing its objective.

Do you plant seeds of hope? Or are you a pessimist who sows despair, doubt, and darkness? Can you see the old passing away and the new coming? Are you willing to give someone the benefit of the doubt, recognizing that the new is coming for him, too? "He who began a good work . . . will continue to perform it until the day of Jesus Christ." What a hope!

> Love knows no fading of its hope (Phillips).

> There is no limit to its hope (NEB).

Love Always Perseveres

Love hangs in there. It doesn't give up. "When love has no evidence, it believes the best. When the evidence is adverse, it hopes for the best. And when hopes are repeatedly disappointed, it still courageously waits."

To persevere is to wait courageously. The root of the word means to wait instead of fleeing, to hold out, to endure. Love cares enough to stay when things are not always going well.

> Love endures all things (RSV).

> Love is the one thing that still stands when all else has fallen (Phillips).

> There is no limit to its endurance (NEB).

Summary

Speaking the truth with perseverance, we will encourage growth.

Speaking the truth with hope, we will encourage growth.

100

Speaking the truth with trust, we will encourage growth.

Speaking the truth with protection, we will encourage growth.

Speaking the truth while rejoicing in the truth, we will encourage growth.

Speaking the truth having forgotten the past, we will encourage growth.

Speaking the truth without anger, we will encourage growth.

Speaking the truth without selfishness, we will encourage growth.

Speaking the truth without rudeness, we will encourage growth.

Speaking the truth with humility, we will encourage growth.

Speaking the truth without boasting, we will encourage growth.

Speaking the truth without envy, we will encourage growth.

Speaking the truth with kindness, we will encourage growth.

Speaking the truth with patience, we will encourage growth.

This is true because:

Love Never Fails.

C H A P T E R

8

LOVE DRIVES OUT FEAR

Talk is cheap. Theory is interesting—and usually quite antiseptic. In real life the trenches beckon. Life itself is quite dangerous. Most people don't get out alive! It's not enough to be armed with fine-sounding words and marvelous platitudes. If the goal is to become more lovable, what specific actions will be perceived as lovable? If you were dragged into court and accused of being lovable, what kind of evidence would the prosecuting attorney present in an attempt to put you behind bars? Would they throw the case out of court for lack of evidence? If you were guilty of implementing the insights of the Apostle of Love as recorded in his first epistle (1 John) they'd send you up for life! John's dangerously practical letter spells it out in black and white. Let's cautiously probe his epistle for our mutual benefit.

Mature Love Drives Out Fear

> There is no fear in love. But perfect love drives out fear, because fear has to do with punishment. The man who fears is not made perfect in love (1 John 4:18).

The words *love* and *perfect* occur together four times in John's epistle. Personally, I don't think *perfect* is the best translation of the original Greek term. *Perfect love* could be better translated *love which has accomplished its task*.

In other words, love has a mission—many missions, in fact. John is saying that when love has finished its work, one result is that all unreasonable fear will have been driven out, eliminated, defused of its power.

Lovers hunt. Bears, bass, birds, and bargains? Sure, all of those things. But that's nothing special: even selfish, uncaring people join hunting parties and fishing clubs. With lovers, it's different. They have a more important quest than filling frying pan and freezer. *They hunt fear!* Their lives are consumed by an never-ending search-and-destroy mission.

Their mission does not lead them to marsh, cornfield, forest, and stream. (Or for that matter, to garage sales and year-end clearances.) Their quarry, their prey, their adversary lurks deep in the recesses of the human soul. The habitat of fear is the heart of man, the inner landscape of his being. A whole catalog of fears haunt, cripple, and enslave.

A Catalog of Fears

Some fear love itself. They gave, were rejected, and withdrew. Used and abandoned, these victims fear risking intimacy again. It's no wonder. Sin-fueled lust often masquerades as love. Trustful hearts crumble as selfish motives inevitably surface through the veneer of contrived compassion. Lust often uses the vocabulary of love to manipulate and deceive. Scarred, disillusioned victims become accomplished fugitives. Dying inside, they withdraw and hide. Many become cynics and despair of life itself. John tells us that love—the genuine article—identifies and devours illegitimate fear.

All expressions of fear are not wrong or unhealthy. To the contrary. We need to fear flames, hurricanes, floods, and consequences of inappropriate and destructive behavior. Not a bad idea to fear breaking the law—whether it be God's law or the law of your city or state. Most fear, however, cripples human potential. Like the fear of failure. Or of the future. Or of growing old, or of children leaving, or of retirement, or of death.

There are a myriad of fears. Innumerable fears. They bite at peace of mind; they blight life's simple joys. Leaving the theoretical behind, let's get to the point. Are you ready? Do others sense your love for them is growing? How would they know? What evidence could they present to demonstrate that your love is increasing? When all else fails . . . read John's directions. Love drives out fear! As love increases, fear decreases. If your friends used such terms as *increased security, confidence, hope,* and *acceptance* to describe the impact of your life, you've got the real disease. You're a hunter of the first magnitude! But let's probe deeper into John's insight.

Do I Produce Fear?

That's the first of three vital questions with which a genuine lover concerns himself or herself. Do I make people fearful? Do I? Ah, that's a crucial question. But shouldn't we expect to be feared or respected? Respected, yes. Respect, however, is earned—not demanded. The outward response to respect on demand may be a joke. The verbal "yes, sir" may contradict true feelings. It could be the only option where fear and coercion dominate. A five-hundred-pound gorilla can sit on any park bench his heart desires.

Follow a fear-producer around for a few moments. When he bursts into a room, an office, or a bedroom, conversation stops. Employees hush, children flee, wives cringe, weep, or become silent and withdrawn. Joy leaves, happiness jumps ship, music and celebration go AWOL. The sun hides its face, the wind holds its breath—as joyless victims walk on egg shells, stomachs churning. Physical, emotional, and spiritual abuse is a regular part of the agenda.

Fear producers wear many hats. Some are legalists—Pharisees in disguise. Fear peddlers can be brutish snobs or Mary martyrs. Most are little people . . . small in patience, little in kindness, stunted in relational sensitivity. They hold grudges, feed closet skeletons, and withhold affection. Sometimes negative and pessimistic, they are usually down on what they are not up on. If murder means to take life away . . . they're murderers who kill slowly. Victims dry up. Personalities change. Spunk, joy, creativity, and beauty fade away as fearmongers hawk their wares.

Lest fear producers be perceived as being monsters, it must be remembered that some people produce fear inadvertently. They've never been made aware of their responsibility to alleviate fear and its crippling impact.

Fear can be a trickling stream or a raging torrent, an unexpected shock or an unwanted companion. Sometimes the sudden, the unexpected is easier to cope with than the persistent, the unshakable. Both bulldozers and beavers can get trees to fall. When bulldozers go on the rampage, the ground shakes, roots moan, tree trunks shudder and splinter, and branches snap like matchsticks. No indeed, you reply, that's not me! I'm no bulldozer! Perhaps not. But are you a beaver? Beavers fell trees, too. But they do it slowly, quietly, relentlessly. And they are very effective.

Is that you? Could it be that you are blind to the damage you're doing in your little forest?

Stop and think, for a moment, how you come across to people. Do you make declarative statements . . . or ask questions?

Do you demand . . . or suggest?

What is your body language saying?

How about your tone of voice?

Are you using size or position to intimidate or manipulate? Do you warn and threaten?

How often do you compliment others for what they do right?

Do you have a tendency to focus on what folks do wrong?

How bad do you have to win?

Do you withhold affection to get what you want?

Are you a bully?

Have you checked your kids' fingernails lately?

Why are they afraid? Of what?

Are you part of the problem? How?

Let's shift gears for a moment. If God is love, what has

he done to drive out fear? Remember that John linked fear and punishment. To stand in the presence of a holy God who demands perfection is not my idea of an afternoon well spent. God's holiness demands that justice be done, sin must be punished. It cannot be overlooked or made light of. The Great White Throne of Judgment beckons. The books will be open, nothing will be hidden, all secrets will become public knowledge ... unless God's love has devised a plan to protect his holiness and extend his forgiveness.

He has such a plan! Christ's love went all the way to Calvary where he suffered on our behalf, paying the penalty for us. Casting out our fear of punishment cost him his life. He became sin for us ... that's love. God's love has acted decisively to eliminate fear.

> Therefore, there is now no condemnation for those who are in Christ Jesus ... (Romans 8:1).

> Therefore, since we have been justified through faith, we have peace with God ... (Romans 5:1).

God's love has acted, it is up to man to respond. If he does, he need not fear being judged by God. His appointment at the Great White Throne is canceled. Christ was judged for him ... that's love.

Should we fear God—in the sense of being in awe of his holiness, power, and all-seeing presence in our lives? Yes, very much so. But it is a *positive* fear—a fear that is rooted and grounded in love.

I was sort of the black sheep of my family. I took many unscheduled flights to the basement where I experienced numerous existential encounters with my father. Believe me, I feared getting my hide tanned. I feared my father at those tense and usually painful moments. And so I should. Such fear is legitimate and healthy. I did not, however, fear being abused, mistreated, neglected, ignored, or condemned. Dad was not a fear producer in the sense that he used size, position, and authority to intimidate, manipulate, or control. I never doubted that he loved me. I never doubted that I had a secure, unshakable place in his heart.

Did I respect his authority? You'd better believe I did! But it was a respect rooted in love.

Are you a fear producer? What *kind* of fear are you producing . . . a healthy respect, or a numbing dread? A mature lover drives out fear.

Do I Perceive Fear?

This is the second key question asked by genuine lovers. It's pretty tough to eliminate what I cannot see. Fear is an elusive master of disguise.

Our culture encourages us to cover our fears. Especially us men. We're trained from early childhood to bite bullets and ride off into sunsets . . . alone. Right? Consequently, most of us are not sensitive to the fears which haunt others. Ask the average man the number one fear of a woman and he'd probably be speechless. In case you wonder, research indicates her greatest fear is the possibility of being used and abandoned. That fear may grow and loom larger and larger as advancing age takes its toll.

As we said earlier, gravity eventually wins! Crow's-feet, adipose tissue, spots, and gray hair gradually alter the human landscape. Aging is especially traumatic for those who have leaned on physical appearance as a passport through life. It's a false security. The younger, smoother, and firmer inevitably arise to edge the older off the stage and claim their brief moments in the sun. But the shadow, the inevitable twilight, will claim them, too. What does a woman need to hear from her lover, her fear-hunting husband?

"Honey, you improve with age!"

As clock and calendar move relentlessly forward, families change. Kids leave, and mom and dad are left alone . . . with each other. The divorce rate shoots upward at this point. An emotional and spiritual separation has often taken place years before. A divorce simply legalizes what has been a reality for a long time. The empty nest is often a mixed blessing. . . a time of fear and uncertainty. Mom often feels her reason for existence—her significance—is slipping away. Dad struggles with his waning youth, the realities of mid-life.

Aging is accompanied by a vast array of potential physical ailments. Surgery, hospitalization, and the death of loved ones are all sources of fear and uncertainty. Financial time bombs tick away in many homes. Money matters. Inflation, devaluation, fixed incomes, skyrocketing costs, increased competition, diminishing markets, bankruptcy, and foreclosure fuel the fires of fear.

Men? Their greatest fear is failure. As younger, hungrier, and often more skilled associates in the vocational marketplace push and shove for their piece of action, fear gnaws at the soul. The fear of failure is the nemesis of many males. I remember the day I was sawing a board in the garage and my wife asked me, "Why are you sawing it that way?" I saw red. Defensive, I asked, "What's *wrong* with the way I'm sawing?" My thoughts? "There I go, I've failed again. Can't even cut a board correctly." An innocent question focused on an incessant need: the need to succeed. The need not to fail.

Kids have their fears, too. Do we perceive them? Many live with the insecurity of feuding parents. An increasing number live in single parent homes, often assuming the blame for the marital disruption. I just heard that in Newport Beach, California, seventy-five percent of the children now live in single parent families. The national average is now forty-six percent. Tear-soaked pillows, wet beds, and chewed fingernails are often symptoms of fear . . . fear that dad's going to leave mom, fear of not being wanted or loved, fear of failing academically or athletically, fear of no support as they face life's problems.

Kids are confronted with such debilitating fears almost every day. My daughter recently asked me, "Dad, are you ever going to leave Mom?" I was stunned. I couldn't believe she asked that question. To say that it bothered me is an understatement. Probing deeper, I discovered that some of her classmates' parents were splitting up. Who knows how long she pondered that question before she asked it. It's possible she shed tears thinking about that possibility. At the dinner table that evening I informed the family that this daddy (me) was never going to leave their mother, period!

Love identifies and drives out fear. Lovers become students of those they love so that they can perceive fear and take whatever steps are necessary to confront it.

Do I Process Fear?

This is the final key question for true-hearted lovers. It's not enough to perceive fear. Love drives it out! Love acts to relieve it . . . if that is possible. Some fears can be eliminated, others cannot. If surgery is inevitable, little can be done to eliminate the reality of pain and discomfort, the uncertainty of the outcome. The lover, realizing he cannot alter these realities, still does all that he can to help the prospective patient process those fears. He prays, he stays, he comforts, he provides, he cares, he protects. In a nutshell, he walks through the pain experience with the one loved.

I watched my son struggle with fear on the basketball court. Temporarily paralyzed by a horrible disease, he had spent many weeks in the hospital. This was followed by months in a wheelchair and endless hours of therapy and exercise. His peers outstripped him in ability, stamina, and experience.

This was his first attempt at basketball. His peers had been playing for several years. As an ex-basketball player, I watched with great anticipation. Finally, in the third quarter, the coach put him in. My son was playing! But much to my surprise and chagrin, Stephen avoided the ball. If a pass came to him, he would return it immediately without dribbling the ball. He camped out on the side of the court away from the ball. He didn't want to touch it.

I was mortified! On defense he was assigned to a very good ball handler. He wouldn't go near him. Consequently, this young lad scored point after point—unchallenged. I couldn't believe it.

Time was called. I rushed onto the court and cornered my son.

"Stephen, you've got to help out your team. You've got to guard your man!"

Tears welled up in his eyes. "Daddy," he said, "I'm afraid."

Of course he was afraid. How stupid could I be? He didn't want to fail. He didn't want to display his inabilities to the general public. So what's a father to do? Eliminate fear? I could jerk him out of the game, out of basketball, out of competition . . . forever. But would that be the loving thing to do? Would that be an expression of seeking his highest good . . . in spite of pain and fear? Sometimes the only legitimate option is to help someone process fear, to walk through it, to face it. It often hurts to heal.

Wracking my brain, I knew I had to find a way to help him walk through those fears . . . to face them and conquer them head on. Quick as a flash it came to me.

"Stephen, I'll tell you what I'll do. Every time you dribble the ball I'll give you a dime. Every time you shoot the ball I'll give you a quarter. If you make it . . . fifty cents!"

He was a new kid. His buddy would throw the ball inbounds to him. He'd stand in one place and dribble. Looking up at me, his eyes sparkled like a fast-moving cash register each time the ball bounced . . . ten, twenty, thirty . . . He dribbled, shot, ran, and guarded. Didn't make any points, wasn't a hero . . . but in my books he was a winner.

Sometimes we have to use all our energy and creativity to help a person process fear. Undoubtedly our physical presence is a great fear-buster. Sometimes there is simply no substitute for *being there*. I like the story of the young boy, awakened from his sleep at night by a furious thunder and lightning storm. Terrified, he ran into his parents' room, dove into their bed, and snuggled up against them. His dad held him close and assured him that he need not worry, God would take care of him.

"I know," the lad replied, "but right now I need someone with skin on 'em."

When I speak of physical presence, it must not be a preoccupied presence where we monitor conversation and beam and murmur at the appropriate spots. Sometimes it's necessary to punch the off button, let the football game fade from the screen, and give undivided attention to the victims of fear. They need to be heard. As insignificant and irrational as the fear may appear to be, it is very real to the one experiencing it. And that reality must be faced.

There are many times when the fearful person isn't really looking for a solution. All he or she wants is simply to have someone affirm the emotion, to say, "It's okay, I understand."

Love faces up to fear . . . and takes appropriate action.

9

LOVE
BUILDS
CHARACTER

The apostle of love isn't finished with us yet! Yes, love takes the initiative to drive out fear. Lovers *are* hunters. That mental picture of Cupid with a bow and arrow has an element of accuracy to it, after all. But lovers are also builders. With God-given tools in hand, they set out to build confidence, an atmosphere of mutual compassion, and an attitude of obedience to the truth. Talk about quality building materials! These are the bricks and mortar and boards and nails that construct eternal character.

John's calm, steady voice rings true after nineteen— nearly twenty—centuries. Like the nerve-steadying voice of an airline captain to turbulence-buffeted passengers, the apostle's timeless words bring assurance, hope, and perspective.

Love Builds Confidence

"Love is made complete among us," John says, "so that we will have confidence on the day of judgment" (1 John 4:17). This is the positive side of eliminating fear. The vacuum left by fear needs to be filled with confidence. When love has completed its work, the apostle is saying, it will have accomplished both tasks—fear will flee and confidence will seep steadily into the inner reservoir.

The primary point of this passage is that God has already acted in such a way that we can have confidence as we face the coming day of judgment. God's love reached all the way to Calvary . . . and beyond. Christ's love expressed itself in taking appropriate action to assure you and me, objects of his love, that we can enter his eternal presence with confidence. Underlying the example of God's redeeming love is the principle that lovers build confidence. God is our model.

So how do you build confidence? By discovering "judgment points." That's the first step. Kristen, my daughter, has a spelling test this Friday. It's a judgment point. She will either face it with confidence or fear. My son has an appointment with the doctor. It's a judgment point. A friend may face a court date, an exam, an interview, an event or circumstance which causes uncertainty, fear, or feelings of inadequacy. A husband may face a significant contract negotiation, a critical business decision, a job interview. All our calendars record regular judgment days when we need others to help us be prepared and confident.

When Kristen has a science test, she needs more than a dad who believes in her. She needs a dad who turns off the TV, puts the book down, rearranges his priorities, and spends time helping her study for her exam. How long does a loving person help? Until he or she is convinced that the individual is ready to face with confidence the demands of the exam, the meeting, negotiation, or whatever it might be. It takes time and sensitivity. What a joy to come home at night and ask Kristen, "Hey, beautiful, how did you do?" I already know the answer by the look on her face . . . and the fact that I hung in there with her until I was sure she was prepared and confident!

When we treat people according to their true value, we are preparing them for achievement, we are establishing the context in which they are most apt to face life with confidence. To value someone is to will his achievement, to strive to assure his success.

Confidence is certainly a primary success factor. To build confidence I must eliminate inappropriate fear. The child who says "I can't" probably won't. The person who visualizes himself to be a failure probably will be . . . unless a lovable person helps him face his fears and pays the price to instill confidence. It doesn't come quickly. It isn't cheap. Ideally, it begins in childhood. The child becomes, to a large degree, what he sees reflected in the face of his parents. A lovable parent is one who visualizes achievement and paints a vivid, enthusiastic picture of future possibilities. My mom always told me I'd make a good surgeon. That seed paid tremendous dividends. It built confidence, it set a standard of achievement. Although God had different plans for me, my mom's confidence continues to make a substantial contribution to my life and ministry.

I'm trying to play the same role for my children. From the time my daughter was a small child she has heard me ask her this question:

"Kristen, you know what excites me about you?"

She knows what I am about to say, but usually she will reply, "No, what Dad?"

"Kristen," I tell her, "you are going to grow up and be a lady. Not every little girl grows up to be a lady, but you are going to."

And you know what . . . she is! We have talked a lot about what it means to be a lady, what it means to be beautiful. When I see her responding like a lady, I say, "See, I knew it, you're becoming a lady." Much of the challenge of building confidence boils down to such seed planting. A child with normal intelligence has the potential of doing well in school, especially if the parent believes he will do well, and communicates this expectation. "Kristen, your brain works so well . . . you're good at figuring out those problems. You're going to enjoy school, you're going to be a good little student."

A lovable person is one who is continually encouraging a person to reach, stretch, seek, and risk.

Howard Hendricks, mentor to hundreds, used to write the most encouraging comments on my assignments when I was his student in graduate school. "Joe, I can't believe they pay me to grade papers like this. WOW!" Or "Joe, you have a way with words, writing should be a part of your future." Who . . . *me*? A green, untested little frog in a giant pond?

Confidence is often a matter of perspective. The glass is either half full or half empty . . . depending upon how one views it. Let it be half full . . . for their sake. The rock-bottom foundation, the bottom line of confidence is trust in God . . . the settled conviction that God is in control of the details of my life. Confidence is not pumping sunshine or gilding the tragedies and sorrows of this life. The confidence builder is ultimately a signpost, a guide who directs others to the ultimate reality, to God, the only source of security and rest.

It is precisely because he has made each day that we can publicly express our confidence by rejoicing. Confidence is an attitude, a perspective based on God's providential care and concern. His love, backed by his promises, assures us we can live confidently. There is no room for gloomy, doubting pessimism in the Christian life. Lots of room for hurt, pain, pressure, and disappointment, but not pessimism! We worry about tomorrow when we forget that he provides for what he values. He never changes. Often our horizontal outlook on life is a reflection of our vertical view of him.

Go for it . . . focus on what those you love do well rather than upon their failures. *Encourage*, don't discourage. *Build*, don't destroy. *Believe*, don't doubt. Try eliminating the scold from your voice, the scowl from your face, the correcting mode from your repertoire of behaviors. Compliment good judgment when it occurs and it will return.

Earlier in this book I mentioned the regular "encouragement reports" I write for each of my children. Why not try something like that? How about a notebook for each child in which you write a letter, a progress report, a confidence builder each month? This gives you a chance to communicate your love in a written, permanent form. It allows you to record significant achievements and important milestones in the child's life. In it you can record memorable events, family activities. It becomes a significant journal, a treasured memory chest. This monthly "epistle" allows you to tell them you love them, you trust them, you appreciate them. It also allows you to remind them that they can count on you to always be there, to back them up, to stand with them, to be on their team. Include two to three prayer concerns which you have for them. Believe me, it will build confidence.

Wife, husband, are you a builder of confidence? Do you encourage, compliment, anticipate down days and pressure points? Are you using some of your time and energy to anticipate judgment points and help others encounter them successfully? Become a confidence builder. They'll love you for it!

Love Encourages Mutual Compassion

"If we love each other," John writes, "God lives in us and his love is made complete in us" (1 John 4:12).

God's love—our model—focuses its energy on helping people love each other. As a third party, he seeks to help me love you or my mate or my friend or my enemy. He is not content until forgiveness flows freely between objects of his love. He is not content until the estranged are reconciled.

It's a tall order, a big challenge to be an agent of reconciliation. Sin predisposes us to hide and hurl. Love's mission is to break through Berlin walls and challenge adversaries to risk reconciliation. Mature believers persist in their love for others, realizing that grudges, bitterness, and unforgiving attitudes and actions deaden and destroy. They've seen vitality siphoned away, joy evaporate, and peace slip out the back door when bitterness settles in.

The decision trail of a lovable person includes some of the following decision points. First, he has seen the futility of "letting the sun go down on his wrath." He's discovered that burying hostility is an exercise in futility ... it doesn't stay buried! Consequently, he cares enough to confront ... to confront his own wrong attitudes and actions.

Second, he is learning to risk reconciliation. He desires to keep short accounts, to deal with differences rather than deny them. Experience has taught him that silence is seldom golden. Third, he has committed himself to live life armed with a clear conscience. Knowing that rationalization is perhaps the greatest enemy of reconciliation, he is willing to call sin sin. Asking for forgiveness is his usual response to personal failure.

Fourth, he freely and graciously extends forgiveness when others wrong him. He resists the temptation to hold out, to seek a pound of flesh, to sulk or play games. Someone has said that "forgiveness is the fragrance flowers give off when they are trampled upon." Attempting to seek relational harmony may get you trampled upon.

Fifth, the lovable person has made a commitment to be a peacemaker, to be part of the solution and not part of the problem. "Blessed are the peacemakers" said the Prince of Peace. The fruit of the Spirit is "love, joy, peace . . ." Peace is right at the top of God's priorities for us.

John is reminding us that the truly lovable person, committed to encouraging mutual compassion, forgoes the luxury of criticism and gossip. He frees others to love and be loved. He is willing to step into difficult interpersonal relationships and seek peace. So, how are we doing? Are we encouraging unity, love, harmony, peace, and reconciliation? Lovable people do. Those developing these skills are increasing their value . . . and their lovability.

Love Aligns Lives with Truth

"But if anyone obeys his word," John continues, "God's love is truly made complete in him" (1 John 2:5).

God's love acts to align lives with truth. Following his example as the source of love, lovable people are continually seeking to direct others toward what is true, real . . . toward reality. Love keeps working, influencing, teaching, modeling, and disciplining until its object perceives, accepts, and applies truth.

Note carefully that the issue is obedience to the truth, not simply the understanding of it. Lest the word *truth* seem overly general, let's call it *reality*. Reality is truth. Love is constantly attempting to nudge its object toward reality . . . as revealed in God's Word.

God has declared his Word (truth) to be of supreme importance. Only those committed to truth have a ghost of a chance of achieving security and significance. God's love is our pattern. Paul tells us to be imitators of God and walk in love. He is our example, our model. Following his example as the source of love, lovable people are continually seeking to direct others toward what is true, real . . . reality. Truth liberates. Shout it from the rooftops. *Truth liberates!* Lovers liberate. They don't possess, imprison, control, dominate, manipulate . . . they liberate. Truth sets free those held in bondage to error, falsehood, and deception.

And liberation is what we need. The god of this world, the old serpent himself, has blinded the eyes of men and women so that they cannot perceive or enter into the joy of building their lives around truth. Unfortunately, seeking security and significance down the wrong path builds momentum toward disappointment and ultimate failure.

Richard Revere, a writer for the *New Yorker* magazine for over thirty years, wrote his memoirs which he entitled "Final Reports." His conclusion, written days before his death in 1979, contains these words:

> If I were applying for employment, I would have to describe myself as having spent the last year staving off death as a fireman puts down flames.
>
> Oh, but I hate it . . . and fear it and find few words that reach the depths of my feelings . . . my character is being altered in ways I find unbearable to record. I seem to myself to become pettier and meaner and more selfish by the hour.

Whatever else may be said, here was a man who apparently went through a lifetime without discovering the liberating truth of the gospel—the good news of forgiveness, cleansing, and change. There is no substitute for obedience to the truth. A life built around error is a tragedy.

Lives are shattered when a lie, a falsehood, or plain old disobedience finally bears fruit. Adultery won't work, cheating doesn't pay, lying will finally catch up with you. We reap what we sow. Truth is the basis of all that is beautiful, wholesome, right, and proper. God's character is the ultimate basis of reality, the very definition of what is true. To live outside the boundary conditions of his holy character is to live an illusion, to build a future on error and deceit. Consequently, truth is perhaps the greatest treasure we can share with those we love. Truth is the heart and soul of love.

Tough love is uncompromising in its commitment to that which is just, right, and true. Love can settle for nothing less than truth. God's powerful love illustrates the fact that genuine love works continuously to align one's life with truth. But don't be deceived. We are not to furrow our brows, rattle our swords, and march forth as defenders of the truth. We're not knights in armor jousting with windmills. Any way you slice it, truth without love is brutality. We are to "speak the truth *in love*" if we would have any hope of producing growth.

Note that although speaking the truth is an act of love, it is to be accompanied by an attitude of love. There is a direct correlation between the assurance of love and the acceptance of truth. If I sense that you genuinely care for me, I am much more inclined to accept the truth you are attempting to communicate. In Galatians Paul reminds us that "the only thing that matters is faith which expresses itself (demonstrates itself) through love (active compassion)."

But there is much more to truth than speaking it. We've got to live it. Seeing is believing. The good Lord commands us to let our lights shine before men that they may *see* our good works, not hear them. He doesn't invite the world to listen, but to look! Paul calls us living epistles, read by all men. When our love is felt, the message is heard. When we practice (obey) what we preach (the truth), the life-giving words come through loud and clear.

God's liberating love will never be satisfied with us until we get beyond knowledge to obedience. To be obedient means to take what I know out of mothballs and live it. Because God loves us, he keeps on loving us toward truth, toward reality.

And it hurts. Truth usually does. That's why most of us

would rather that God just be kind to us, not love us. "Forget making me a masterpiece, Lord. Just make me a thumbnail sketch and tape me to the wall."

It's the same principle within the family. Love costs something. It would be much easier just to give up on your kids. What difference does it make whether they learn to obey or not? Who cares if they rebel, break the law, violate the rights of others, destroy themselves? Wouldn't it be less hassle just to let them do what they want, when they want, where they want, how they want? Quite frankly, if personal comfort and absence of pain were the goal, we would probably choose not to love. When we say, "This hurts me more than it hurts you, son" . . . we understand something of the place of pain in the process of love. Sometimes it's painful to align someone's life with the truth. But if we love, we'll do it anyway.

Moses' instructions to the generation about to inherit the promised land helps us visualize something of the process of getting truth into life. He understood the balance between truth taught and truth lived when he commanded the moms and dads of his generation to teach and talk about the great truth of loving God supremely. Effective education involves the formal and the informal, the classroom and the living room.

The process of communicating truth begins with the heart of the parent. "These commandments that I give you today are to be upon your hearts" (Deuteronomy 6:6). If it's only in the head, forget it. The biblical model moves from the heart to the home. "Impress them on your children. Talk about them when you sit at home and when you walk along the road, when you lie down and when you get up. Tie them as symbols on your hands and bind them on your foreheads. Write them on the doorframes of your houses and on your gates" (Deuteronomy 6:7-9).

Another translation of *impress* is to "teach them diligently." The focus of this word is a formal, structured exposure to God's word. The verb is used in other places of sharpening a knife, scythe, or sickle by repeated, laborious whetting. We all need a repetitious, regular, formal exposure to God's Word. Sunday school, church, and family altars provide opportunities for systematic instruction. Every morning and evening my father, riding herd on nine children, led the family in a time of Bible study and prayer. I still marvel. I guess we can always do what is important to us, no matter how formidable the odds!

Unfortunately, however, the formal is often not enough. A steady diet of doctrine may leave a person spiritually starved. Thousands sit, soak, and sour . . . attendance pins and all.

No, the teaching of truth is not to be limited to the four walls of the classroom. It is to be talked about, discussed, and debated when we walk, sit, lie down, and get up. Life's most crucial curriculum is taught in the home. Moses instructs us that parents are to serve as interpreters of life, injecting truth into the events and circumstances of everyday living.

Our forum is not so much the podium, the chalkboard, the overhead projector. It is the office, the water cooler, the lunchroom, the ball field, the dinner table, the bedroom. Truth is best taught in the context of life.

The Lord allowed his disciples to be the center of attraction when he fed the hungry multitude. The outsiders sat while the insiders served. What a sight that must have been! I imagine it must have been mighty impressive to be one of the Lord's associates—one of the inner circle—as hundreds of people marveled at Christ's power and authority. It would have been easy to get puffed up with importance, to forget the reality of the situation, the true meaning of events. So what happened immediately after that?

Ah, there's nothing like being in a small boat during a violent storm at sea to teach humility. Things were brought back into perspective with telling force. Storms teach. Storms make us teachable. God arranges the circumstances of everyday life so that sensitive instructors can use these teachable moments for redemptive purposes.

From the heart to the home to the habits. Moses says love hasn't accomplished its purpose until truth is obeyed, until it expresses itself in action. "Tie them [the commandments] as symbols on your hands and bind them on your foreheads. Write them on the doorframes of your house and on your gates" (6:8-9). Our actions (hands), thoughts (foreheads), homelife (doorposts), and business life (gates of the city) are to be regulated, controlled by obedience to the commands of God. Lovers move loved ones toward obedience to that which is true. If we love God, we obey him. It's as simple as that. God loves us and insists that we obey. He uses circumstances, events, people, suffering, and joy to move us toward obedience. As we become absorbed with the truth about his holiness, love, and grace, we grow in our desire to do his will . . . to obey.

The greatest thing I can do for another person is to woo him into obedience to truth. God has no plan B. His call to obedience is irrevocable. Every knee will bow.

John's counsel helps. Lovable people hunt fear, build confidence, encourage compassion, and promote obedience. Put these four actions of love somewhere near the top of your priority list. As you do this, remember, everything good will be attacked. Don't let pressure deter you from what is honorable, what is right, and what is pleasing to God.

10

LOVE'S
PILGRIMAGE

The new birth launches us in the direction of authenticity, a biblically informed conscience keeps us heading toward it, and our growing sense of value gives us permission to accept love and the ability and freedom to express it. As we grow in him, we grow in our ability to decrease fear, build confidence, encourage mutual compassion, and align lives with truth. Valued for these contributions, we are loved, we are perceived as lovable—we make it easier for others to love us.

Our love also becomes the key to making other folks lovable.

It could take a long time.

It could be very difficult.

This is where the biblical concept of *agape* love comes into play. We're talking about tough love. We're talking about loving the other when there isn't much to love. We're talking about lots of giving and not much receiving. But remember, lots of giving may prime the receiving pump! A trickle of love may start in your direction. It may. Hearts still follow value. Value tugs, it perks people up, it captures attention.

Dough on the Axe Handle

There's no denying that the unresponsive, unloving object of our love often becomes a burr under our saddle blanket. We'd like to drop kick them out the door. You know what I mean? It's tough, isn't it, to fly like an eagle when you're living with a turkey . . . a Ford instead of a Cadillac! I know. But the bottom line is still love . . . and at times love in spite of what they are and how they act.

Lovable people act in loving ways not because they always feel like it or even perceive value in the object of love. They do it because of commitment. It is commitment that holds a relationship together between the periods of love. In this day of wash-and-wear wedding dresses, we live in the midst of a people who are long on romance and short on commitment. You mean I'm stuck with him? I think that's what I mean.

That thought makes me think of the elderly lady in southern Georgia who was busy kneading a batch of bread dough. Noting that her old wood stove needed replenishing, she hastily pulled her hands from the dough and scurried to the woodpile where she split an armload of firewood. Returning to her kitchen, she reloaded the cook stove.

Her teenage granddaughter turned to her and said, "Gramma, how long does the honeymoon last?"

"Till there's dough on the axe handle, honey," the old lady replied, "till there's dough on the axe handle."

Resisting the obvious comments about old battle-axes, it suffices to say that marriage duets do become duels. An old Arab proverb says that marriage begins with a prince kissing an angel and ends with a bald-headed man looking across the table at a fat lady. The dough does get on the axe handle. Plato is reputed to have said, "By all means marry. If you find a good wife, twice blessed you'll be. If not, you'll become a philosopher." The quote is probably apocryphal, but freighted with significance nevertheless. What happens to all those lovable people? Makes one wonder if there is life after marriage.

Dough or no dough, one had best not assume love will make it through courtship into marriage.

Few know what love is—much less how to love. Love is often perceived to be a sun-splashed, honeymoon-flavored emotion, a sort of ecstatic paralysis fueled by romantic nonsense of every sort. This pink-cloud feeling survives intact during that period of simulated perfection we call

126

courtship. But let the dough get on the axe handle—and it will—and marital compatibility becomes for many the impossible dream.

Marital compatibility? That's part of the pink cloud myth. Marriage is really the process of working out *incompatibilities*. The term *process* implies time and motion (force). Fueled by an awareness of value, love is both the motivating force and the set of behaviors which pursue the resolution of these incompatibilities. Lovable folks carry oil cans, not sandpaper. When I was a teenager my mom sat me down and shared some invaluable counsel. "Joe," she said, "some day you will wonder if you married the right person. You will wonder what it would be like to be married to someone else." She was right. "The key," she went on to say, "is commitment. You will learn how to love." She was right again. I've been learning ever since. I'm a full-fledged supporter of the wise soul who stated that "a marriage license is just a learner's permit."

Let's be honest. The folks we really love . . . are those who love us. Depending on the nature of the relationship, we perceive such people as close friends, lovers, sweethearts. In these cases love has reached its highest level, that of warmth, friendship, mutuality, and intimacy. Rich indeed are those who sustain a dozen such reciprocal friendships. Most of us treasure the few who perceive us as valuable—and long for more. By and large, in this sin warped world, we're commissioned to love those who don't have us high on their priority lists . . . and turn them into lovers.

How Do We Do It?

Good question! Lovers spend much of courtship trying to tie the knot and most of their married life trying to untie the knots and snarls which each brings to the relationship. Lovers untie knots . . . theirs and others! We've looked at the knots of fear, lack of confidence, lack of social skills, and the knots produced by error and the abandonment of the Cross Walk. On a positive note, lovers help fulfill the two basic needs of security and significance. But to charge off scattering love in all directions at the same time may prove to be an exercise in futility. We need a roadmap, a set of tracks to run on, a schema, some signposts along the way.

Can love be charted, dissected, and broken down into its component parts? Maybe. Love does seem to move through some identifiable, definable stages which are helpful in determining where we are—and where we need to go—in a given relationship.

The Stages of Love

It's hard to know where to go if we don't know where we're at! Without perspective, we hang on pegs suspended securely in midair. Appropriate action is impossible without adequate direction. Here are some signposts to try on for size.

The First Stage of Love: Information

It all begins with facts (at least we think they are facts). Our scanner scans the romantic landscape. Green lights and red lights flash. Suddenly the thing goes wacko. Ninety-five percent of the lights are green. Bright green. Someone has captured our attention, jammed our circuits, crashed our computer. We're hooked.

What started as rational has become irrational. Facts have been transformed into fantasy. We like what we see. We've seen lots before, but somehow this one is special, this one registers, this one storms the heart. Infatuation strikes hard. We seek more information, and blinded by ecstatic paralysis, it too comes up green.

In a recent "Nancy" comic strip, Sluggo's friend tells him that he is truly in love. Sluggo says, "Oh, really?" "Yeah," he says, "Now all I have to do is find a girl." He's in love with the idea of love. One's idea of love often determines the nature of the data that registers.

Love really is three dimensional, having three essential and necessary components: *eros*, *philos*, and *agape*.

Eros is love determined by some value or attribute outside the person doing the loving. It may be an attractive face, a well-proportioned figure. Eros generally grows out of the nature of the object. "Love is 36-24-36." Nothing wrong with that if it is balanced and controlled by the other two dimensions. Two mutually infatuated people can want each other desperately without love, and without sensing the emotional insincerity that plagues them. By and large, *eros* seeks in the other the fulfillment of its own life hunger.

Bodies are in! Some of my best friends have them. But we don't fall in love with a body, we fall in love with a *person*. Scripture teaches that love is the larger component of which sex is but one part. Marriage is not licensed prostitution! Folks who use their bodies as bait may attract lots of attention, but they seldom attract genuine lovers. Though often mistaken for love, erotic enchantment usually visualizes the other as an accessory rather than as an individual. Flattery, glamour, and social excitement are usually substituted for realism.

So what's wrong with a little romance, a little flair, a little appreciation of the sexuality of the other? Nothing, as long as it's balanced by healthy doses of *philos* and *agape*. One can't read the creation account or the Song of Solomon, for that matter, and miss the point that physical intimacy was God's idea.

Philos is the love of mutual companionship and friendship. It has all the overtones of a warm kitchen, a crackling fire, hot cider, good music, and a special friend. It's a sharing, "warm puppy" side of love. This is the goal, by the way, of all love. It's a reciprocal, mutually beneficial type of relationship, the ultimate goal of lovable people. Those individuals want people to love them because of what they are. They work hard at increasing their value and making it easier for others to love them. It is to be hoped that phase one lovers (eros) will become friends (philos).

Agape has none of the power or magic of *eros* or the warmth of *philos*. It does not love because of the lovableness of the object. That's *philos* love. *Agape* is unmotivated by anything outside of itself. It's tough love, as we saw earlier. It loves in spite of the nature of its object. It is a decision to act—with little or no expectation of reciprocity.

Eros says "I want you, I need you." Philos says "I enjoy our mutual admiration society, and the benefits which accrue to it." Agape says, "Because God has commanded me to love, and because you have objective value as an image bearer of Almighty God, I will commit myself to your highest good . . . even if I don't feel like it." The ultimate good, remember, is to treat someone according to his true value, *whether or not that value has become actualized*!

Notice that each dimension of love is based upon information. Eros focuses on the package and accepts or rejects the person on the basis of external considerations. As *philos* develops, it responds to those nuances of warmth, companionship, spiritual oneness. Agape looks heavenward for marching orders, and otherward for needs to be met. Self is subordinated to the needs of others . . . for Christ's sake, and Christ's sake alone.

Disappointment and disillusionment in marriage often grow out of the primary focus of courtship. If the focus was primarily *eros*, it often becomes very difficult to develop those higher values of warmth, companionship, and spiritual oneness. Many marriages begin with *eros*, move toward *philos*, and then end. Eros alone is not a sufficient marital glue. The good ship "Eros" won't keep many marriages afloat.

That is not to minimize the importance of *eros* in the lives of couples who are drawn together, come together, and stay together. By no means! Most such unions begin with more than adequate doses of *eros*. But they also go some distance toward becoming friends. If they don't quite reach that goal, their commitment to God, to themselves, and to each other is strong enough that they roll up their sleeves and get about the business of learning how to *agape* each other until the friendship factor begins to flower. The marriage stays together and grows as each partner skillfully responds with appropriate portions of *eros*, *philos*, and *agape*. We never outgrow our need for all three dimensions of love!

Information lights the fuse . . . and extinguishes it. We feel good about a person because our thoughts are good.

We are processing "good" information. Our emotions are the products of how we think. Courtship is primarily a green light period. Not many yellows and reds show up on the instrument panel. Just positive information, positive thoughts, positive emotions. After the encounter at the altar, however, altercations follow the inevitable alterations. Red and yellow lights suddenly appear.

Could we have married the wrong person? Help! We'll change 'em. That's the secret. Believe me . . . it isn't. I don't want to be your project, and I'm sure you don't want to be mine. Subtly, almost imperceptibly, our focus changes. The green lights fade from our field of vision. That value-pursuing heart seems to be focusing in new directions, seeking new treasure. Am I just another toy in his toy chest?

Three Steps to Love Recovery

Negative thoughts produce negative emotions. The erotic enchantment wears thin as reality seeps into the relationship. Bit by bit, practical values fade. Attention to the aesthetics of body and spirit slips, and resentment builds. So how do those who have lost their first love recover it? The Lord's directives to the Church at Ephesus are quite instructive.

> I hold this against you: You have forsaken your first love. *Remember* the height from which you have fallen! *Repent* and *do the things you did at first* . . ." (Revelation 2:4-5).

Three simple steps: *remember, repent*, and *do the things you did at first*.

Remember

To remember is to recreate events and circumstances from the past. It is to reprogram your computer with long-forgotten data. It is to shift focus from the present time of disharmony back to a past time of care, compassion, and tenderness. It is a call to evaluate the present in the light of the past to determine direction and correction. Remember all those green lights, this passage teaches, so that the red lights of the present can be seen in perspective. Sure, some of the green lights have gone out, but they can be switched on again. A fair amount of the red lights shine because of *your* red lights. Punch out a few of them and perhaps your mate's reds will diminish too.

Paul could say, "if anyone is in Christ [a Christian], he is a new creation; the old has gone, the new has come!" Do you see the old passing away and the new coming? Sometimes we must take it by faith, but that's what *agape* love is all about! The insights in this portion of Revelation are crucial. Proper emotions follow proper thinking. The folks at Ephesus had gotten so caught up in the mechanics of defending the faith, in arguing for orthodoxy, that they lost their love for the Lord. Recovering lost love involves recovering lost and overlooked data. It means overcoming our tendency to focus on what is wrong, and focus instead on what is right.

It wouldn't be a bad idea to take a piece of paper and a pencil and list all the things that are right and good about that mate, that child, that parent, that peer.

Repent

You've made the person a prisoner of the red lights.
You haven't given him or her the benefit of the doubt.
You've been overly critical.
You have not been affirming.
You have established unbalanced priorities.

All of these things are wrong! To repent of them means to change your mind, to adopt a new course of action, a new set of priorities, a new perspective. How can tug build if you ignore positive data? If you refuse to treat your mate according to his or her true value? If you refuse to love in spite of red and yellow lights?

Do the Deeds You Did At First

Can you remember them?

Remember again those special dates. Open car doors for her. Put notes in his suitcase. Fix his favorite meal. Take her to her favorite restaurant. Be fit for her. Get into better shape for him. Don't sit and wait for an erotic emotional tornado to fly through your living room. Modern research confirms that if you will perform the actions of love, *the feelings will follow*.

It is not enough simply to go on an archaeological expedition into the past to recover lost and ignored data. The Bible has more than enough to say about our responsibility to love, and this data needs to be rethought and reprogrammed into the computer. Loving the wife is not a suggestion. Nor is accepting the leadership of the husband, or obeying the parents. A rereading of biblical data is never a bad idea.

Throw it all in the hopper . . . the memories of the past, of courtship, of those early days, those precious moments, the failures and successes . . . and the biblical commands and imperatives. Repent. Do. Do, whether you feel like it or not. You say, "I'm a hypocrite to act loving toward him when I don't feel like it." Not so! It's never hypocritical to do what God has commanded you to do whether you feel like it or not.

One of the most frustrating experiences in life is to feel that you have been evaluated and rejected on the basis of biased, limited data. You want to break through, to present new information, to feel like all the facts have been carefully weighed. We fail, and often make genuine efforts to start afresh . . . and aren't allowed the privilege. We hear, "Yes, but . . ." and die inside. Our fresh determination goes down the drain as we are haunted by another closet skeleton. Let there be new beginnings, let there be the luxury of failure.

Love begins with information—facts colored by our needs, focus, expectations, and sexuality. To continue in love is to continue in the process of responding to all the pertinent data. To continue in love is to forget the past, to celebrate new beginnings. To continue in love is to repent and do. Lovable people convey the impression that they make every effort to be current. They look to the future and see the new coming.

The Second Stage of Love: Acceptance

Jennings's Corollary states that "the chance of bread falling with the jelly side down is directly proportional to the cost of the carpet." He's probably right. All good will be attacked. It's inevitable. Lovable folks accept jelly on the carpet. It's one thing to be current and up-to-date on all the facts. It's quite another thing to let go of the negative facts, to refuse to use them as ammunition, to accept the reality of imperfection and failure.

Acceptance says:

> It's okay for you to be you. You're not my project, a prisoner of my expectations. God is not at war with your humanity . . . neither am I. The work God has begun, he will perform according to his schedule, using his means.

But what about our imperfections, our blemishes and warts? As C. S. Lewis put it, God loves us in spite of our imperfections, but never ceases to will the removal of those imperfections. To love another person is to care deeply about the growth and development of all his human powers and abilities. I can care deeply and still be relaxed about the process. "It is God who works in us, both to will and do of his own good pleasure."

So how do you communicate acceptance? Frankly, you can't hide it. Your mate knows quite clearly whether or not you accept her or him. The first struggle is internal, isn't it? You have to bury your resentments, your hurt, your crushed and exaggerated expectations, and come to terms with the reality of the marriage relationship. In an "instant everything" age, I guess most aren't prepared for the life-long dimensions of the process. We must kiss the "if onlys" goodbye. Be done with them! They serve no useful purpose. Some dwell forever on what might have been. Forget it. Learn from the past and then *leave it*. Remember, your mate is probably equally disappointed. Look to the future. Place your hope in God and hang on.

Love begins with information. Take an inventory of what you have. Review again your biblical responsibilities.

Express your acceptance and appreciation to your Heavenly Father. After all, that mate of yours is God's responsibility. To continue to question the desirability or suitability of a spouse is ultimately an insult to God. If you are willing to concede that as far as you are concerned this is your mate as long as he or she lives, you will find acceptance to be much easier. Acceptance of the permanency of the relationship precedes acceptance of the partner. If it's permanent, sooner or later you'll go to work and build it. If it's permanent, sooner or later you will accept your mate. If there is doubt about permanency, we focus on the red lights because we are looking for justification for abandonment.

Have you settled in for the long haul? Your mate will know it.

Have you abandoned your attempts to make him or her over again? Your mate will know it.

Have you quit comparing, playing the field, fantasizing about others? Your mate will know it.

Have you traded in your correcting mode for an affirming one? Your mate will know it.

Pats, touches, and embraces sprinkled liberally throughout the day will get the message across. If you're moving toward *philos*, you're on your way.

The Third Stage of Love: Approval

It's one thing to come to the point of acceptance, it's quite another thing to express approval. Many accept but don't approve. In such cases, acceptance is really resignation. "I'm stuck with him, guess I'd better accept him and get on with it."

Approval is the word *prove* with an alpha prefix. It means "I don't have to prove anything." What a liberating thought. I'm not on trial, don't have to jump through anyone's hoop, I've got the Good Housekeeping Seal of Approval. Approval means granting your partner full rights to his or her unique personhood. How can I love you if you seek to enslave me?

Have you ever communicated the fact that you approve of your mate, your friend, your companion? Do they feel like they don't have to be on guard when they are around you? Does your tone of voice express approval or disapproval? Disapproval is a powerful weapon which parents sometimes use to control kids. Kids learn fast and carry over many of these patterns into adulthood. After all, can you imagine *your* reaction if your wife or husband were to grab you by the chin, turn your face, and unleash a blast of disapproval right between your eyes? It would be a little hard to handle, wouldn't it?

Remember the buckets we discussed in an earlier chapter? One bucket, you'll remember, was marked with a big plus (+) sign. The one in the opposite hand was marked with a minus (—) designation. Lovers fill and fill and fill the approval bucket. Believe it or not, even disapproval can be expressed maturely and in a productive manner.

Lovable folks are loved because they are affirming. They look for what the person does right, what he does well, and express their approval. People are made to feel secure and significant. In a nutshell, lovable people believe in people. Don't you want and need someone to believe in you? I do. I especially need my wife's approval. Thank God she gives it!

This does not mean a blanket approval of all that a person is and does. As the old saying goes, "when two or three are gathered together, someone spills his milk." Approval is a growth-stimulating attitude. The approving person is quick to see those positive qualities, the attempts to please, the demonstrations of good judgment, and affirm them. People who have an approving way about them are generally perceived as lovable.

The Fourth Phase of Love: Appreciation

Appreciation comes from a Latin term meaning "to value." In contrast to admiration, appreciation generally focuses on what a person *does*. Do you really appreciate your mate, that friend, that associate? Do you recognize their value and respond appropriately? If the answer's no, then perhaps you need to go back to square one—the informa-

LOVE'S PILGRIMAGE

tion stage—and get all the facts.

You say, "I think I do appreciate my hubby!" Fine. Does he know it? That's the bottom line. It's one thing to be appreciative, it's quite another thing to communicate appreciation. It's in the *communication* of acceptance, approval, and appreciation that we generally fall short.

Really, it's not all that complicated. A large part of it is simply remembering to say thanks. It's being sensitive to the danger of taking another for granted. We all need daily doses of appreciation.

If a person fixes a lovely meal . . . tell her you appreciate it. If an individual makes a schedule adjustment to accommodate you, tell him what that means to you. If a child expresses a mature attitude toward a disappointment, an unforeseen event, take her aside and express your appreciation. If a child behaves well at a restaurant, express your appreciation. Should the child do a decent job of making his bed, don't take it for granted. Express your appreciation . . . regularly. If the kids don't perform as you'd hoped, how about saying (without nagging or scolding), "When it's convenient for you, I would appreciate it if you would make your bed." Every child has the right to be treated with dignity.

Sometimes a gift . . . something tangible . . . is a great way to share your appreciation. This is especially true if the gift is not part of a birthday or anniversary celebration. Instead, it's totally unexpected, it's totally spontaneous. Appreciation is powerful. It can actually direct the growth and development of another . . . especially if that individual knows he is loved.

Appreciation is simply positive reinforcement. As such, it helps an individual know how to behave and gives him a clue as to what is acceptable behavior. As someone has put it, "the reinforced response returns."

The Fifth Stage of Love: Admiration

As a general rule, admiration focuses on what an individual *is*. It is not unusual for mates simply to tolerate each other, knowing little of mutual appreciation and

137

admiration. Some appreciate the meals, the clean clothes, the paycheck. A smaller number actually communicate that appreciation. With a fifty percent divorce rate, one wonders how many of those who stick it out have ever come to the point of admiration.

I suspect that some folks have a very inadequate admiration inventory. Dr. Howard Hendricks used to remind us that we have raised a generation of debunkers, a cadre of people who are always putting down things and people and institutions. Whatever else one might say, such folks are not generally perceived as lovable.

When I find myself around such people, I want to confront them and say, "What are you *for*, anyway? What do you admire, what do you believe in, what is *right* about that person or this world?" These are the ones who drive through the countryside and only see the highway ahead of them. They litter the verbal landscape with such phrases as "So what?" . . . "Who cares?" . . . or "Big deal!"

Love is a skill, an art. We must learn to see, to take inventory, to approve, appreciate, and admire . . . until it becomes second nature. Until we reach that point, we would be wise to keep tabs on how often and when, where, and to whom we have expressed approval, appreciation, and admiration.

Admiration comes from a Latin root meaning "a wonder, a miracle." To be an admirer is to be caught up in the wonder and miracle of another's being. It is to treat him according to his true value. How about a mutual admiration society! Think of the special gifts and abilities that your friend has, and simply tell him you really admire him for those reasons. Is he sensitive to people? Tell him you admire him for that. Does she have the ability to listen? Tell her you admire her for that. Can she handle difficult circumstances with courage and grace? Tell her! Is that child especially tenacious? Does hubby take charge? Does wife do a bang-up job of running the house? Is she thoughtful? Is he fun to be around?

Do you share your admiration of your wife, husband, friend with others? Does your secretary know that you admire your wife? How about your business associates, your buddies, your children? If you're serious about developing a lovable life style, learn how to admire and communicate that admiration.

The Sixth Phase of Love: Adoration

We've left a whole lot of people behind at this point. The road we're traveling is much narrower and "few there be that go upon it." Love involves adoration? I've got to adore him? My husband? Surely you jest. Not really. Love's purpose is to call forth beauty. If you have really loved him through the years, he should be more and more adorable. Peter's secret is quite supportive of this truth. A spiritually insensitive husband can be turned around by a wife who cultivates inner beauty. God says men treasure it, they are attracted to it, they will search out its roots. If they value it, their hearts will feel the tug.

To adore means "to address a prayer to." Woven into the idea of adoration is the concept of worship. It has overtones of that which is sacred, set apart, holy. As I said, not many reach this stage of the pilgrimage. Yet we should. Is not that husband an image bearer of mighty God? Does he not partake of the divine nature if he knows Jesus Christ? Has he not been "crowned with glory and honor" . . . by God?

How would I treat others differently if I really believed they were image bearers of God himself? Could intimacy become sacred communion?

We're walking on holy ground here. We're considering the potential for those few who walk in purity, who are in intimate fellowship with God. Adoration springs from the carefully cultivated soul, from the heart that beats in cadence with God's heart. Adoration is a combination of reverence, respect, and awe.

To those who adore, sarcasm is unthinkable. Would you ridicule that which is sacred? Would you be cruel to something you treasure? Could you ignore and be indifferent toward a choice gift from God himself?

Those who arrive at this threshold have worked hard,

have forgiven much, have accepted inadequacies, have expressed appreciation, and have communicated admiration.

Notice carefully that love begins with facts (information) and moves toward feeling (adoration). When feelings have gone, the goal is not to sit around and wait for them to return. Remember! Repent! Do! Turn from counterproductive patterns, and start doing those first works.

You'll increase your tug and leverage others toward becoming more lovable.